TRAVELS IN TOWN.

BY THE AUTHOR OF

" RANDOM RECOLLECTIONS OF THE LORDS AND
COMMONS," " THE GREAT METROPOLIS,"
&c. &c.

IN TWO VOLUMES.

VOL. I.

LONDON:

SAUNDERS AND OTLEY, CONDUIT STREET.

1839.

CAMBRIDGE LIBRARY COLLECTION

Books of enduring scholarly value

Printing and Publishing History

The interface between authors and their readers is a fascinating subject in its own right, revealing a great deal about social attitudes, technological progress, aesthetic values, fashionable interests, political positions, economic constraints, and individual personalities. This part of the Cambridge Library Collection reissues classic studies in the area of printing and publishing history that shed light on developments in typography and book design, printing and binding, the rise and fall of publishing houses and periodicals, and the roles of authors and illustrators. It documents the ebb and flow of the book trade supplying a wide range of customers with products from almanacs to novels, bibles to erotica, and poetry to statistics.

Travels in Town

Born in 1802 in Elgin, James Grant first established himself as a reporter and then as a leading newspaper editor in Victorian London, heading the Morning Chronicle for two decades before moving on to the Christian Standard. His 1839 Travels in Town was designed as a companion piece to his earlier reflections on London, The Great Metropolis (1838) and Sketches in London (1838). This two-volume work reflects Grant's enthusiasm for 'this modern Babylon' and his lively interest in the intricacies of everyday life there. Volume 1 focuses on central London, observing major streets (including Downing Street) and the British Museum. Interweaving general descriptions with specific local information, Grant even provides his readers with details of the famous museum reading room and how to access its treasures.

Cambridge University Press has long been a pioneer in the reissuing of out-of-print titles from its own backlist, producing digital reprints of books that are still sought after by scholars and students but could not be reprinted economically using traditional technology. The Cambridge Library Collection extends this activity to a wider range of books which are still of importance to researchers and professionals, either for the source material they contain, or as landmarks in the history of their academic discipline.

Drawing from the world-renowned collections in the Cambridge University Library, and guided by the advice of experts in each subject area, Cambridge University Press is using state-of-the-art scanning machines in its own Printing House to capture the content of each book selected for inclusion. The files are processed to give a consistently clear, crisp image, and the books finished to the high quality standard for which the Press is recognised around the world. The latest print-on-demand technology ensures that the books will remain available indefinitely, and that orders for single or multiple copies can quickly be supplied.

The Cambridge Library Collection will bring back to life books of enduring scholarly value (including out-of-copyright works originally issued by other publishers) across a wide range of disciplines in the humanities and social sciences and in science and technology.

Travels in Town

By the Author of Random Recollections of the Lords and Commons, etc.

VOLUME 1

JAMES GRANT

CAMBRIDGE
UNIVERSITY PRESS

CAMBRIDGE UNIVERSITY PRESS

Cambridge, New York, Melbourne, Madrid, Cape Town, Singapore,
São Paolo, Delhi, Dubai, Tokyo

Published in the United States of America by Cambridge University Press, New York

www.cambridge.org
Information on this title: www.cambridge.org/9781108009126

© in this compilation Cambridge University Press 2009

This edition first published 1839
This digitally printed version 2009

ISBN 978-1-108-00912-6 Paperback

PREFACE.

THE title of this work may at first sight seem inappropriate. It has been chosen because the volumes contain the results of a very extensive intercourse on the part of the Author, with the inhabitants of this modern Babylon, and of an intimate acquaintance with many of its most interesting institutions. The book is intended as a companion to "The Great Metropolis" and "Sketches in London," and if it only meet with as great success as these two works have done, the Author will have abundant reason to be satisfied with its reception by the public.

LONDON, *November*, 1838.

CONTENTS OF VOL. I.

CHAPTER III.

TATTERSALL'S AND THE TURF.

CHAPTER IV.

DOWNING STREET.

CHAPTER V.

THE BRITISH MUSEUM.

CHAPTER VI.

THE BRITISH MUSEUM—(CONTINUED).

CHAPTER VII.

THE NEWSMEN.

TRAVELS IN TOWN.

CHAPTER I.

THE STREETS.

Leading entrances to London—Streets near St. Katherine's
Docks—Cheapside—Streets in the vicinity of the Elephant and Castle — Piccadilly— Oxford Street—Gower
Street — Mile-end Road — Whitechapel — The People in
the streets — Difference in the appearance of different
streets — Interesting associations connected with particular
streets—The streets as they appear by day, and as they
appear by night—General remarks.

THERE is nothing that so forcibly strikes a
stranger, on entering London, as the state of its
leading streets. When I use the term street, I
shall not, I am sure, be understood as meaning
the pavement or causeway of our principle
thoroughfares. I refer, if the expression be a

proper one, to their animated condition, as illustrative of the character, habits, and pursuits of
the inhabitants of our compact metropolitan
world; for London must be regarded as a little
world of itself.

There may be said to be, just now, seven
great openings into London, through which the
vast majority of visitors make their entrance
into it.   The first is through Gracechurch
Street or King William Street, into the city.
Through one or other of these streets, most of
those who come by sea to London, whether
from some part of the United Kingdom, or from
some more distant part of the world, enter this
all-absorbing place.

Another road is that which, passing the
Elephant and Castle, extends itself to the
High Street of the Borough, and thence along
London Bridge to Gracechurch Street.   A
third, is that which comes past Hyde Park
Corner, and loses itself in Piccadilly.   These
roads connect the metropolis with various parts
of the South of England.

A fourth great opening into London, is through

Oxford Street, the longest, and perhaps the
finest street, all things considered, in the world.
This is the inlet to the metropolis from the
Western parts of England, as may be inferred
from the fact, that on the passengers arriving at
Paddington, from the Great Western Railway,
they, with very few exceptions, proceed to Oxford Street, and then are swallowed up in this
mighty metropolis.

The fifth great entrance into London, is
at Euston Square, the terminus of the London
and Birmingham Railway. This is one which
is of recent origin. Twelve months have
not elapsed since this opening was made,
and yet it has already become one through
which immense numbers of people daily thrust
themselves into the heart of this metropolis.

The sixth is through the great North Road,
which may be said to terminate at the Angel
Inn, Islington; for from that place large and
commodious thoroughfares branch off in every
direction; so that not only the stranger, but
even the person who has been many years resi-
dent in London, feels himself in some measure

lost when in that particular spot. To be sure, the number of persons entering London from the great North Road has of late very considerably diminished, owing to the partial opening of the London and Birmingham Railway ; and when the work has been completed, and the trains shall run all the way, the number of persons who will come to the metropolis through Islington will be still further reduced.* There is no doubt, however, that the great North Road must continue for many years to be one of the principal entrances into London, as it leads directly to various towns of considerable population and importance.

The seventh, and last, of the principal openings into the metropolis, is by Mile-end Road. This is the thoroughfare through which nearly all persons, coming from the East of England, make their entrance into London, and as none of the railways have yet interfered with it, it continues to pour a constant stream of human beings into the all-absorbing vortex of this vast place.

---

* Since this was written, the railroad has been opened all the way.

Reverting to the opening into the metropolis, first mentioned, as that through which almost every person who travels by sea, is obliged to pass; it is one which is perhaps more calculated to make an impression on the mind of the visitor than any of the other six. On the river after he has reached Blackwall, all is bustle and confusion. The vessels which are stationary, coupled with those which are sailing to or from a part of the river nearer the heart of the great city, are objects of intense interest to him. His attention is diverted from them by the innumerable shoals of skiffs and other boats which are plying all around him. Nothing could so much rivet the attention, and excite the astonishment of the stranger, on his first voyage up the river, than the innumerable boats and vessels of every kind, which meet his eye in all directions. He is amazed at the rapidity with which some of the lighter craft skim along the water, and wonders that, with their number, and the celerity with which they are propelled, accidents so rarely occur. All is animation, and bustle, and business; the river is a place of extensive traffic; on a fine day it has all the appearance of a fair.

But this is a digression. My present subject is the streets, not the river. If the stranger land at St. Katherine's Docks, his first impressions of London, after he has got into the nearest streets, must be exceedingly unfavourable. The houses are high, and dark, and dingy; the streets are narrow, and it is a hundred to one if they be not wet and dirty; for a clean and dry street in the immediate neighbourhood of St. Katherine's Docks, is indeed a rare circumstance. There are no signs of commerce, except it be here and there a solitary cart loaded with merchandise, lazily wending its way towards the city. The streets are nearly deserted, and the stranger not only wonders that people could be induced to live there, but he begins to be incredulous as to all he has heard of the bustle, and business, and fine appearance of the streets of London.

The route, after landing at these Docks, will most probably be through the Minories, where he will see a pleasant, open, respectable-looking street; but still there is nothing in it which at all approaches his ideas of London. He enters Aldgate, and proceeds in the direction of Corn-hill, and then he begins to think with himself, that this is the metropolis of which he has heard so much. If he land in the vicinity of London Bridge, he wends his way, under the direction of some cabman or porter, until he reaches Gracechurch Street, or King William Street, and then, all at once, a new scene bursts on his gaze. There he is confounded by the signs of life, and activity, and business which meet his eye, and which also appeal to his ear.

At whatever part the visitor may have landed, he is sure, if his place of destination be in the centre of the metropolis, to pass through Cheap-side. And then what a scene opens to his view! Not more astonished could he feel, had he been suddenly transported into another planet. Every thing is new and surprising to him. He is overpowered with the sight. The pavement on either side is crowded with pedestrians, not walking leisurely, but *hurrying* onwards on their respective errands, and to their respective

destinations. On the pavement on the right
hand, you see one great and continuous stream
of human beings, rushing, if I may use the expression, in a westward direction; another stream
of men and women is running in an eastward
course. On the pavement on the other side,
you also see two similar streams — perhaps,
torrents would be a more expressive word—of
human beings, running in an opposite direction, and yet the one stream never interfering
or coming in collision with the other. The
stranger cannot fail to be much struck at the
entire absorption of every one he sees, with
his own matters.

The teeming population on the pavement
all pass each other with as much indifference
as if they had not eyes in their heads, or
were so many inanimate objects moved by
machinery. They seem as if they did not
belong to the same species, or as if it were a
crime to take cognisance, in any way, of each
other, as they pass along. The middle of the
street again is so crowded with vehicles of every
description, that Cheapside often appears one

vast coach-stand. So closely are the vehicles here sometimes pressed together, that you have to walk a considerable distance before you can cross to the opposite side.

In an article on the vehicles of London, which I wrote some time ago for a popular periodical, I mentioned what every one acquainted with the metropolis knows to be a fact, that so great is the number of vehicles sometimes to be seen at one time in Cheapside, that could a person scramble along horses' backs as well as over the tops of coaches, cabs, carts, omnibuses, &c., he might almost pass from one end of that street to the other, though more than a third of a mile in length, without once putting his foot on the ground. What the astonishment of the stranger must be when he sees so great a number of vehicles of every class, and almost all containing persons proceeding from one part of London to the other,—will be better imagined than it were possible for me to describe it. Once through Cheapside, it is unnecessary to follow the stranger further. Nothing he sees in the city will strike him as wonderful, after he has passed along that crowded and ever-active thoroughfare.

The entrance to London in the Elephant and Castle direction, is one which has its objects of interest to the stranger, though such interest is not so great as that which attaches to the entrance just referred to. The " huge town" comes more gradually on him. He is prepared for a place of great population, and great traffic by the crowded state of the suburbs, and the immense number of vehicles of every description which are flying about him in all directions. He reaches the Elephant and Castle, and is confounded by the number of stage-coaches, all full of passengers, which are either resting for a moment to put down or take up customers, or are being driven with an alarming rapidity along all the great roads which branch off from that particular point. He is astonished that, where there is so much furious driving in thoroughfares so densely crowded as are all the leading streets in that immediate neighbourhood, there should be so few accidents, either through vehicles coming in collision, or through

pedestrians being run over. When once past
the Elephant and Castle, on his way to the
Borough, the visitor may be said to have entered London. The High Street of Southwark
has much of the bustle and animation and trade
of the leading thoroughfares on this side of the
water. He is surprised at what he sees,—at
the splendour of many of the shops, and the
crowded and animated appearance of the streets;
but the surprise comes on too gradually to be,
as in the case of a sudden entrance into Gracechurch Street, or King William Street, of an
overpowering kind.

But by far the most striking and imposing
entrance into the metropolis, is that by Hyde
Park Corner, and along Piccadilly. The
crowded state of the road, both with vehicles
and pedestrians, as he reaches this end of
Knightsbridge; the handsome houses on the
right-hand, and the park on the left, are well
adapted to prepare him for the great vortex into
which he is about to plunge himself.

Proceeding a little further, he finds this wide
and open entrance into London much more

thickly studded with vehicles of every description, and more crowded with pedestrians. He
reaches Hyde Park Corner, and his eye is
arrested, first, by the great extent of the Park,
and then by the splendour of the entrance into
it. He turns to the right, and sees another extensive and beautiful park, also boasting a magnificent entrance. His attention is withdrawn
from these by Apsley House, the town residence of the Duke of Wellington, which, it is
worthy of observation, is the very first house
on the left hand of Hyde Park Corner, and,
properly speaking, the first house on entering
London from the south of England. Splendid
mansions on the left now challenge the visitor's
attention for a considerable distance, while on
the right he looks through the Green Park
for about a third of a mile, until his eye is
arrested by Buckingham Palace, the residence
of our popular maiden Queen. Is it not a magnificent structure? Is not the Green Park a
beautiful place?

He proceeds on his journey through Piccadilly, utterly lost in astonishment at the scene of

activity which presents itself to him. The
pavements are bending under the crowds of
pedestrians, for the most part elegantly attired,
who are hastening to their several places of
destination ; while the middle of the street appears one vast assemblage of vehicles driven at
a rapid rate. He is struck with the great
number of noblemen's and gentlemen's equipages which here mingle with the common
hackney coaches, omnibuses, &c., and forms at
once in his own mind some conception, though
but a faint one, of the luxury as well as of the
business and bustle of this metropolitan locality.
Stage-coaches and omnibuses whirl past him in
such rapid succession, and all so heavily laden
with passengers, that he cannot help fancying
that London is in the act of emptying itself of
its population. He cannot conceive how such
crowds of people could continue for any length
of time to hurry out of town without draining
it of its inhabitants, and leaving it a comparatively desolate place. The farther he proceeds, the more is he convinced of the un-
tenableness of his theory; for as he reaches

the White Horse Cellar, which is about half
way down Piccadilly, he finds to his unspeak-
able surprise, that the streets instead of
being thinner, are more and more crowded.
He feels as if he were in a new world. He
cannot comprehend how business can be carried
on, or how people can exist with any comfort
to themselves, in a place where the pavements
are so thronged with people—the streets with
horses, carriages, gigs, cabs, omnibuses, and
every description of vehicle—and where there
is an everlasting deafening din, and a confusion
which, as he thinks, could not be surpassed.
In whatever direction he afterwards proceeds,
provided he keep by the leading thoroughfares,
he finds so much of the same noise and bustle
and confusion, that he gradually begins to
cease wondering at it.

The entrance to the metropolis from the
West end of Oxford Street, is well calculated
to give the visitor a favourable impression of
the place. The moment he enters it, he is struck
with its fine open appearance; but especially
with its great extent; for it is about a mile

and a half in length, in a straight line; being,
as already remarked, longer than any street
in any other city in the world. He is amazed,
if not overwhelmed at the scene before him;
for the whole of this space, extensive as it is,
appears as if it were one mass of life and animation. The pavements, as in all the other
principal thoroughfares in London, are so
densely crowded with pedestrians, that you
wonder how they manage to move with such
alacrity. The middle of the street, as in Piccadilly, exhibits an incredible number of vehicles
of all descriptions—from the most splendid carriages of the aristocracy, down to the coster's
donkey and cart. Perhaps, with the single
exception of Cheapside, there is not a street
in London through which so many vehicles
pass: of omnibuses alone, no fewer than 1200*
run along it every day. When the stranger

* I need hardly say that I do not mean, that there are so
many separate vehicles; for that is a greater number than
there is in London. I only mean, that including the return
of the same omnibuses, and the third and fourth journeys
they often make in the same day, 1200 journeys are accomplished in the course of twelve hours.

passes Regent Circus, his attention is withdrawn in part from the crowd of pedestrians
and vehicles, to the splendid shops which present themselves on either side, but especially
on the north side of the street.

Altogether different is the first impression
which a stranger has of London, when he enters
it at Euston Square, the termination, as before
mentioned, of the London and Birmingham
railway. If he proceed through the squares in
a south-east direction, he is struck with the
aspect of elegance and comfort which they
present; but there are no indications of his
being in the first commercial town in the world.
If he take the more direct road, which is along
Gower Street, to the centre of London, he finds
himself for at least a mile of his journey, to be
passing through a street which scarcely exhibits any signs of its being an inhabited place.
Here and there you see a solitary pedestrian,
or perchance a one-horse chaise. The stranger,
in passing along this street, feels an emotion of
melancholy come over him caused by its dulness
and unbroken monotony; and fancying it, per-

haps, to be a fair specimen of London, he wonders how people can betray so entire a disregard of the truth as to represent the metropolis as a place of business and bustle, and noise and din. His notions of London are rectified when he reaches High Holborn. If he see few or no traces of splendour there, both his ears and his eyes admonish him of the traffic and animation of the more central streets of the metropolis.

The entrance by the great North Road, has nothing of peculiar interest until you reach the Angel Inn. Then the stranger begins to fancy, from the stir and bustle, and the number of omnibuses and persons moving in every direction, that he has got into the great Babel. Still he has no definite notions about the place. He sees but few shops, and these few are only of a very inferior kind. If he look down the City Road, the houses all appear clean and comfortable, with small gardens before the doors of the majority of them. If he cast his eye in the Pentonville direction, the aspect of things is pretty much the same. If he look forward, or towards the south, he sees only small houses,

not much calculated to inspire him with any
very exalted ideas of London. Whatever direction he takes from this particular place, he
finds that he must proceed at least a mile
before he can reach a spot which will afford
him a fair specimen of what the leading streets
of the metropolis are.

The other great entrance into London which
remains to be adverted to, is that at the East
End, along the Mile-End road. The number of
persons who daily enter this mighty metropolis
at this point, is very great, though I am not
able to furnish any idea of what the actual
number is. The buildings in this direction
extend so far, that the stranger fancies he must
be at the farther end of the town, before he can
well be said to have entered the place. He has
travelled at least two miles and a half, during
which time, he has concluded that he was in
the very heart of London, before he has reached
the eastern extremity of the city. In Mile-End
Road he has seen vehicles without number, with
swarms of human beings : he has seen stands on
the outside of the pavement, as well as shops in

their usual places, for the sale of every conceivable article which a person could be supposed likely to wish to purchase. He concludes that this must be a fair specimen of the general aspect of the metropolis. He enters White-chapel, and proceeds along it in the usual way, and is surprised at the altered appearance, as compared with that of Mile-End Road, which presents itself to his view. He sees nothing on the south side but sheep and other animals, slaughtered for the good of man. Inwardly, he inquires, can we be a community of fleshers? Of this he is certain, that Buonaparte would have been nearer the mark, had he characterized us a nation of butchers, instead of a nation of shopkeepers. To be sure, the error is but of a very transitory duration, for he has only reached Aldgate when he discovers his mistake. There he has the first indication, though an imperfect one, of what he may expect our principal metropolitan thoroughfares to be.

Such are the leading entrances into London, and the aspect of the streets or roads in which they are situated. The longer the stranger remains in town, the less striking, of course, do the streets appear to him. The gloss of novelty, as a necessary consequence, gradually wears off; but, after all, there is always something in the appearance of our principal metropolitan streets to interest and amuse. The bustle and activity, at all times observable in them, is one feature, which cannot fail to keep up the attention of the passer-by. Then there is the display of human character which is always to be witnessed in the streets. You not only see around you every variety of human character, but you often see eccentricities of character displayed to the greatest advantage. You see the fop as vain of his figure, or, more properly speaking, of himself, as a peacock is of its gaudy plumes of feathers. By way of contrast to him, you see men literally stooping from their bashfulness or humility. There is the perfect dandy; yonder is a man who cares nothing about the decoration of his person. That man on your right is a habitual swindler, and lives by plundering his fellow men; the person on his left would rather die of hunger than defraud any individual under heaven, of even a farthing's-worth of property. That person, who walks at so quick a pace, is an active man of business, and has now something which bears on the interests of the shop on his mind; the individual who is nearest to him, and who is pacing the pavement so leisurely, has nothing to do, or rather will do nothing except live in idleness at the expense of the public or his friends. In fine, you not only see every variety of human character, as you perambulate the streets of London; but you often see peculiarities of character exhibited to the greatest advantage; for all being here equally buried in the general mass, individuals have fewer conventional restraints laid upon them.

Not more marked is the difference in the appearance of the streets themselves, in one part of London, as compared with the streets in another, than is the difference in the feelings, habits, and manners of the persons who walk along them. In Cheapside, or the other leading thoroughfares in the city, the individuals you find perambulating those thoroughfares are

altogether different in every thing but form and
stature and the attributes which are common to
human nature, from those you meet in Regent
Street.   In Cheapside every one seems bent on
some errand of the deepest importance; or, on
some matter of business which will admit of no
delay.   Time is precious to him; you see the
man of trade or commerce visibly imprinted
on his face.   He has, most probably, a good
coat on his back, but there is nothing of the
dandy about him.   His wardrobe exhibits no
traces of having " come through the hands" of
some of the fashionable " decorators" of the
West End; in his case, you cannot say with
truth, that the tailor makes the man.   There is
nothing stiff or artificial about him; he has
not time, far less the disposition, to play the
fine gentleman.   But very few of Truefit's customers find their way to the city.   To see a
moustached personage in that locality would
excite our special wonder.   Were we to meet
with such a rarity, one could scarcely help
" taking a note of it," with the view of putting
it in print.   A walking-cane is also an article

very seldom to be witnessed in the hands of a
city pedestrian.

Behold the contrast in Regent Street! The
patronizers of that fine, open, beautiful street
are evidently there, for the purpose of seeing or
being seen. You perceive, by their physiog-
nomies and manner, that they have nothing to
do; and, in this very interesting way of spending
their time, the one keeps the other in countenance. See what dandies they are! The obligations of the gentlemen to their tailors, and of
the ladies to their dress-makers and milliners,
are too manifest not to be at once observed.
Witness their stiff and artificial gait, and observe how slow and stately are their movements.
What their objects are in being there, beyond
that of wishing to "show off," nobody can
divine; it is doubtful whether they could tell
themselves. Of moustaches we have here a
most abundant harvest; and, as for walking-
canes, and the other usual appurtenances of
sprigs of fashion, their name is legion: they
meet your eye everywhere. The display of
jewellery about their persons is all that could

be wished; it would make any Jew's eye
glisten, as the homely phrase has it, to witness
the number and variety of their "ornaments of
gold." The citizens laugh in their sleeves at
the fashionables of the West End, and the latter
hold the cits in as great contempt as if they
belonged to an inferior order of creation.

Those who know anything of the people of
London, as well as of London itself, must have
been often struck, in passing along its streets,
with the vast difference there frequently is between the appearance of a person's circumstances
and the reality. You meet with men who are
dressed in the extreme of fashion, and whom
you would suppose, judging from their manner
as well as their apparel, to be persons of splendid fortune, who have not a farthing in the
world, and who are often at a loss to know
where or how they are to procure their next
meal, provided they get one at all. In other
cases, especially in the city, you occasionally
meet with persons in the streets, whom you
would fancy, from their wardrobe and general
appearance, could not command a sovereign,

who are worth their thousands and tens of
thousands. Appearances are proverbially de-
ceptive. I know of no instance in which the
adage applies with so much propriety and force
as in that of many of the persons you encounter in the streets of London.

London contains about 8,500 streets, lanes,
&c. Among such an immense number, there
must necessarily be a great variety in their appearance. Some, as has been already more
than once stated, are all life and animation,
and bustle; while others are usually so desolate in their aspect, that it is refreshing to
see some five or six individuals in them at a
time. There are several streets in the metropolis which exhibit so few appearances of life,
that you would have difficulty in persuading a
stranger that the houses were inhabited. Some
streets are open and airy; others are so close
and confined, that you wonder how human
beings can breathe their atmosphere and yet
survive. Some streets are exceedingly beautiful; others are ugly beyond the possibility of
description. There are some you could wish

never to quit; there are others you could wish
never to enter.

In passing along the streets of the metropolis,
there are many interesting circumstances connected with particular places which, were they
generally known, would afford much gratification
to the stranger, apart from the mere architec-
tural appearance of those streets.   For example,
with how much greater interest would the visitor
look at Whitehall, were the particular house
pointed out to him, at the front of which Charles
the First was executed?   Leicester Square, too,
would have additional attractions to any man
who was informed of the house, in that square,
in which Sir Isaac Newton lived.   Even Grub
Street, in Cripplegate, formerly proverbial for
the number of poor authors who vegetated in its
garrets, would be a street of special interest to
every intellectual man, were it generally known,
which it is not, that in one of the houses in that
street, Milton spent several years of the latter
part of his life.

The pedestrian, who has his eyes about him,
as he passes along the streets of London, will

observe many things, unconnected with the mere streets themselves, or the objects he sees in the shops, which will possess considerable interest to him. For instance, he will find, from a notification to that effect above the door of a tobacconist's shop in Newgate Street, that the business now carrying on in that shop, was established in the year 1686, two years prior to the Revolution; which business has been regularly carried on in the same premises since. This is a curious fact, and cannot fail to give rise to a train of interesting reflections. There is another business, that of a pawnbroker in Brydges Street, Strand, which has been carried on unremittingly since the year 1704. But the oldest established business in London with which I am acquainted, is that of a chemist, in King Street, Cheapside. It commenced in 1616. What changes have taken place in London, the country, and the world since that time!

The expedition with which erections are made, and removed in front of the houses in the leading streets of London, at a time of some great public spectacle, is truly astonishing. A few

days, for instance, before the coronation of Her
Majesty, in June last, wooden and other erections of the most substantial kind, started up in
front of hundreds of houses along the line of procession, with a rapidity which, to strangers, must
have appeared almost magical.   But still more
expeditiously did they vanish : in two or three
days after the coronation there was not a trace
of them to be seen.   The streets had as entirely
resumed their wonted appearance as if nothing
had happened.

The contrast between the streets of the metropolis, as they appear in the day and at night,
must have struck everybody.   In the day-time,
the pavements teem with human beings, and
the causeway with horses; all is bustle and
activity, while your ears are assailed with the
everlasting rattling of vehicles.   At night, the
pavements are deserted, and the silence which
reigns around you, is only broken, at long
intervals, by the noise caused by the wheels
of some solitary coach or cab.   But more striking still, because more sudden, is the change
which takes place in the appearance of the

streets when, what the newspapers call a " tremendous shower" of rain suddenly takes place.
The rapidity with which the streets are then
thinned of their pedestrian population, is almost
incredible. The most densely crowded thoroughfares present in a few moments the appearance of
a desert. The marvel is, where the tens of thousands you saw but a moment or two previously,
could so promptly have found a place of refuge
from the pelting rain.

Walking in the streets of London is almost
at all times disagreeable. There is rarely any
alternative between dust and mud. You are
either in danger of being suffocated with the
former, or being covered with the latter. The
suddenness of the transition from being im-
mersed in clouds of dust, to being spattered
from top to toe with mud, is remarkable; it is
what no person living in a provincial town, can
have any conception of. When you come out
from breakfast in the morning, you cannot
cross any of the leading thoroughfares, unless
where some knight of the broom has made a
pathway for you, without being up to the ankles

in mud; in the afternoon the dust is flying in
every direction, in such quantities, that you are
afraid of being choked by it.

The streets of London afford a fine specimen
of a miniature republic. All are there on a
footing of perfect equality. You cannot dis-
tinguish the haughty aristocrat from the humble
mechanic, unless, indeed, you perceive a difference in the cut or quality of their respective
coats. Both pass on equally unheeded by the
crowds around them. The nobleman is unknown,
and would be unnoticed even were his person
identified. No one would pause to pay him
any marks of respect. How different from what
he is accustomed to witness where known in
the provinces! There everybody takes off his
hat to him, and otherwise expresses his respect; here he is utterly lost amidst the crowds
which surround him.

31

CHAPTER II.

THE PARK.

*Its history—Purposes to which it was formerly applied—
Its beautiful appearance—Is the resort of the beauty and
fashion of the Metropolis—A question asked and answered
—The place it occupies in fashionable volumes—Intrigues
in the Park—Love sometimes inspired in the Park—An
instance given—The Park during a sudden shower—Contrast in its appearance at different times—Aristocratic
notions about the Park.*

HYDE PARK, or *the* Park as it is generally
called, to indicate its superior celebrity as compared with any of the other parks in London,
is a place of which every one has heard, and
which every one who visits the metropolis
makes a point of seeing. And yet, notwithstanding the attractiveness of this locality,
there are few persons who have any knowledge

of its history. In my researches into scarce
works of an antiquated date, with the view of
acquiring information respecting the former
history of particular parts of the metropolis,
I have often had to complain of having laboured
in vain; but in no instance have I experienced
so much difficulty in my endeavours to ascertain the history of any institution, building,
or locality, as I have done in my inquiries into
the circumstances under which Hyde Park came
to be what it now is.

The earliest authentic particulars I have been
able to obtain regarding this interesting locality,
represent it as having been seized among the
crown lands soon after the death of Charles I.
It was one of the few royal demesnes which
were excepted from sale by a legislative ordi-
nance issued in 1649. In three years afterwards, it was determined on by the government of that period, that Hyde Park, with
some other lands belonging to the crown, should
be sold for ready money. To what special
purpose the purchase money was to be applied,
I have not been able to learn. Immediately

prior to the sale, which took place in 1652, a survey of the Park was made, and the admeasurement was given at 620 acres. The estimated annual value of the mere land was £894 13s. 6d., which, speaking in round numbers, may have been equal to £3000 of our money. The timber growing in the Park was valued at £4779 19s. 6d., and the deer at £300. The Park was divided into lots, and was sold to various persons. The entire amount of the purchase money received for it, including the timber and the deer, was £17,068 6s. 8d. The crown lands having been resumed by the king immediately after the Restoration, Hyde Park was again replenished with deer, and was enclosed by a brick wall. The Park was at this period much more extensive than it now is. It then extended on the east to Park Lane, and on the west included the space now called Kensington Gardens. Its present extent is nearly 400 acres.

Hyde Park, it would appear, was originally appropriated to all sorts of diversions on the part of the inhabitants of London. A writer

c 5

who flourished about the middle of the seventeenth century, speaking of Hyde Park, as it
appeared on the 1st of May, 1654, says, " This
day was more observed by people going a
Maying,* than for divers years past. Great
resort to Hyde Park ; many hundreds of note,
coaches, and gallants in attire, but most shame-
ful powdered hair men, and painted spotted
women. Some men played with a silver ball, and
some took other recreation, but not his High-
ness the Lord Protector, nor any of the Lords
of the council." It would appear from this,
that Cromwell and his lords of council had been
in the practice of frequenting Hyde Park for
the purposes of relaxation from the cares of
government, if not of diversion. But we are
not left to mere inference on the subject ; for it
is a well known matter of historical fact, that the
Protector, or Usurper,—whichever the reader
according to the complexion of his politics or
his particular views of the history of that
period, is pleased to call him ; it is, I say, a

---

* That is, to celebrate the 1st of May, a custom now only
observed by our metropolitan chimney-sweeps.

well known historical fact, that about this time Cromwell met with an accident in Hyde Park, which was likely to have been attended with fatal results. While one day taking an airing in the Park, he was suddenly seized with a desire to enact the character of Jehu, and accordingly mounted the dickey, and took into his hands the reins which guided the six horses which drew his chariot. He had not long played the part of charioteer, before he discovered that it was somewhat more difficult to govern his six horses, than it was to keep in subjection the twelve or fourteen millions of human beings who acknowledged his sway and submitted to his pleasure. The horses became unmanageable, and the result was, the overturning of the carriage. In Cromwell's fall, one of the loaded pistols which he always carried in his pockets went off, and he miraculously escaped receiving its contents.

Among the diversions which were practised in Hyde Park about the middle of the seventeenth century, that of hunting matches seems to have been very common. " The Moderate

Intelligencer," a daily paper of that period,
says under the date of May 3, 1654, that a few
days before, there " had been a great hunting
match between fifty Cornish gentlemen on the
one side, and fifty on the other." The same
journal adds, that the Lord Protector, and
several of his privy council were present on the
occasion.

Five years subsequent to this, a Frenchman,
writing to a friend in Paris, gives a description
of Hyde Park, which throws some further light
on the uses to which it was then applied. " I
did," says the Frenchman, " frequently ac-
company my Lord N—— into a field near the
town, which they call Hyde Park; the place
not unpleasant,—and which they use as our
course, but with nothing of that order, equipage
and splendour,—being such an assemblage of
wretched jades and hackney coaches, as, next
to a regiment of carmen, there is nothing ap-
proaching the resemblance. This Park was,
it seems, used by the late king and nobility
for the freshness of the air, and the goodly
prospect; but it is that which now besides all

other exercises, they pay for here in England,
though it be free for all the world besides;
every coach and horse which enters bringing
his mouthful, and permission of the publican
who has purchased it; for which the entrance
is guarded with porters and long staves." The
language of this French writer is somewhat
elliptical, but it may be fairly gathered from it,
that Hyde Park was at that time chiefly the
resort of the lower classes, and that some small
sum was exacted from every person who entered it.

The next information of any importance
which I have been able to procure respecting
Hyde Park, is contained in a little work entitled "The Circus; or British Olympics, being
a Satire on the Ring at Hyde Park." From
this work, which was published in 1709, it
would appear that the Park was at that time
the resort of all the fashionable part of the
metropolitan population, and that it was no
uncommon thing to see one thousand carriages
in it in the course of one afternoon.

From 1709 up to the present time, the Park

has continued to be the great resort of the
fashionable world. It is certainly a charming
place. It is in a fine, open, airy situation and
what with the trees in Kensington Gardens, and
the handsome houses on the east, and north,
and south, presents a remarkably interesting
and pleasant view. The entrance to it from
the west-end of Piccadilly is imposing and
magnificent in the extreme. Its attractions,
indeed, altogether are so great, that no other
place in the vicinity of London can bear a
moment's comparison with it. I question if
there be many such places in the world.

If any one would form a correct conception
of the luxury and grandeur of fashionable life
in the metropolis, he must visit the Park on
a fine afternoon, in what is called the London
season. That season usually commences immediately after the Easter holidays, and ter-
minates in July. It is at its height in May and
June. Let, then, the man who is desirous of
knowing something of the splendour of aristocratic life in this mighty place, visit Hyde Park
about five o'clock on a fine afternoon, in either

of those months, and he may be assured that
however high his expectations on the subject
were, they will be far exceeded. He will be
dazzled with the magnificence which surrounds
him. He will be overpowered with the brilliancy
of the scene. He will feel as if he had been
suddenly translated into a new world; or as if
his vision was more than realizing all that he
had ever read, in the pages of romance, of eastern
splendour. As far as his eye can reach along
the carriage-road, he sees nothing but the most
magnificent equipages: their number, not less
than their grandeur, fills him with amazement.
His admiration is divided between the carriages
and those who are in them. Here he sees the
beauty and fashion of the metropolis to far
greater advantage than he could in any other
place,—always of course excepting Almack's,
and some of the great routs which are given by
the Duke of Devonshire, the Duke of Northum-
berland, the Duke of Buccleuch, or some of the
other leaders in the aristocratic world. I speak
within bounds when I say, that if you take up
your station in the middle of the Park, you may,

on occasions, see at one time four or five hundred carriages, phaetons, cabriolets, &c., to say
nothing of single horses, with their noble or
honourable riders on their backs; all whirling
and galloping about with a velocity that gives
to the whole scene much of a fairy aspect.

And is there nothing but happiness in all
this? The man who looks not below the sur-
face of things would come to the conclusion,
that if there be true felicity in the world, that
felicity must be enjoyed by those who revel in
the splendour he sees around him. There could
not be a greater error. Gaiety and grandeur are
not synonymous with happiness. The greatest
luxury and the utmost magnificence will often be
found associated with the deepest misery. The
most gorgeously attired, and highest titled lady
among the vast throng, may be actually much
more unhappy than the poorest mendicant who
crawls from door to door, and whose wardrobe
is a mass of rags. If there be places in the
earth in which the appearance and the reality
are the antipodes of each other, it is in those
places which are the resort of the fashionable

world. You are struck with the singular beauty
of many a lady-face you see around you : there
may be no indication of a mind ill at ease in
that beautiful face; there may, on the contrary, be an expression of cheerfulness, and yet
that expression may be assumed. The bosom
of its fascinating possessor may be the seat
of inexpressible wretchedness. If the higher
classes have sources of enjoyment peculiar to
themselves, they have also causes of misery
which are unknown to those in the lowlier
walks of life. Envy at the real or imagined
better fortune of their acquaintances—the actual
or fancied slight—the constant rivalry to out-
shine each other, and the consequent effects
of this foolish passion—the embarrassment in
pecuniary matters which necessarily results from
those extravagant habits which are generated
by a vain desire for display, and the amours,
intrigues and scandal, which are so characteristic of the aristocratic world, all conspire to produce prolific misery among those whose destiny
it is to live, and move, and have their being in
that narrow and exclusive world.

The Park, as a matter of course, figures largely in all fashionable novels. To write indeed a fashionable novel, without the name of the Park frequently occurring in it, would be held to augur the unfitness of the author for the task he had undertaken. It would at once be set down as a conclusive proof, that the author knew nothing of aristocratic life, and consequently could not be qualified for producing a fashionable fiction. The writer who introduces the Park with sufficient frequency into his work, is at once set down as one who has mixed largely in aristocratic circles, and is well fitted for describing fashionable life.

That the Park should be frequently referred to, and be often made the scene of incidents in the higher circles, is not surprising, when it is remembered how often romantic incidents do actually occur in that interesting, and, in the estimation of the aristocratic world, classical locality. Many clandestine assignations have taken place there. Many are the instances in which the language of love has been spoken by signs in the Park, when circumstances prevented the parties giving utterance to their sentiments by means of the human voice. Lovers in the higher ranks of life are there, in the habit of interchanging expressive glances with each other when they are debarred from private interviews together. Innumerable are the intrigues which are fostered and "advanced a stage" in the Park, in cases where the lady is, as they suppose, so narrowly watched by her friends, as not even to have an opportunity of bestowing a glance on her lover. The colour of a lady's ribbons in her bonnet, the circumstance of her hand encased in a white or other complexioned glove, resting on the window of the carriage, are matters which, though unintelligible to the multitude and even to friends, are found to prove an exceedingly expressive language where the parties, either through conversation or correspondence, have previously had an opportunity of understanding each other.

It were well if the Park were not the means of encouraging anything but pure, even though in many cases clandestine, love. Unhappily it is far otherwise. Innumerable are the guilty

amours which have there been fed and fostered.
Looks and signs have been interchanged between the parties, which, though perfectly unmeaning to, even if observed by, others, have
been most expressive in so far as they themselves were concerned.   I could refer to instances of this kind which have eventually
come before the public, but no good end could
be subserved by a reference to former crimes
long since forgotten.

Young ladies would require to be very careful
how they look and how they act in the Park.
The want of this circumspection on the part
of ladies, and especially of marriageable ladies
with large fortunes, has in repeated cases
been attended with very inconvenient results,
both to the love-struck swains themselves,
and to those ladies whose attractions of face
or fortune have inspired the tender passion.
A very striking instance of this occurred within
the last few months. A week or two before
the coronation of our youthful Sovereign, one
of the richest heiresses, if not the richest
heiress either in England, or in Europe, chanced

to bestow a look on a stranger who was at
the time playing the part of a pedestrian
in the Park. Very likely the lady slightly
smiled on the occasion; for one has no idea of
an amiable and accomplished young lady looking on any one, far less a handsome young
man, without deigning to smile. At all events
the love-struck swain laid the flattering unction
to his soul, that the lady did favour him with
an *Angel*-ic smile; a position in the tenability
of which he felt additionally confirmed when
he saw her drop her glove. There could be
no doubt—so at least he thought—that this
must all be the result of a deep-rooted affection for him, and therefore in the spirit of true
gallantry, he not only felt bound to pick up her
glove, but to lay siege to her hand, as he fancied
her heart was already quite secure. He accordingly became desperately enamoured of the
young lady's self—or fortune, and followed her
in the character of a willing slave, until, at a
favourite watering-place, he allowed his love to
get the better of his discretion, and frightened
the object of his idolatry from her propriety;

making himself not only the subject of fashionable conversation of a very unpleasant kind, but of very ugly newspaper paragraphs.

Perhaps a more ludicrous scene is not to be witnessed, than that which the Park exhibits when a heavy shower of rain overtakes the pedestrians at the season of the year and the hour of the day at which it is most largely attended. And I may here observe, that on a fine Sunday afternoon, the attendance of pedestrians must often be from 20,000 to 30,000. These chiefly consist of dashing young dress-makers, clerks, shopmen, &c., most of whom are attired, as the police reporters have it, "in the extreme of fashion."

Fancy then the terror caused among such persons, when St. Swithin takes it into his head to pay an abrupt and unexpected visit to the Park. Off they set as simultaneously for the nearest houses, in the hope of there finding shelter, as if fire instead of water were descending from the clouds. They look as affrighted as if, instead of fleeing to save their silks and satins, their Saxony cloth, and other fineries,

they were fleeing for their lives. According to
the couplet—

"Those now run who never ran before,
And those who once did run, now run the more.''

And truly laughable is it to witness the way
in which some of them do run. No description
can convey any idea of the variety and awk-
wardness of the positions assumed by the biped
racers. Prim misses and stiff artificial dandies
of our own sex, are compelled to throw aside
for the time all their airs and affectation, and to
take to their heels with all the expedition they
can achieve. Many in the precipitancy of their
retreat have great difficulty in retaining their
equilibrium; others lose it altogether; thus not
only realizing the old proverb of "most haste
least speed," but also converting bad into worse.
When showers of rain do take people in the
Park by surprise, they are usually that class of
showers which the penny-a-liners denominate
"tremendous." And frightful is the destruction
of finery which is the necessary result. Many of
the articles of ladies' apparel never afterwards
recover from the visitation; they cannot be

worn again. The same may be said of the more
fanciful portions of the dress of dandies belonging to the masculine gender. No wonder that
with such probable calamities before their eyes—
to say nothing of their abstract unpleasantness
apart from all future consequences — there
should be a desperate rush in the direction of
the fancied places of shelter. And wonderful is
the alacrity with which the pedestrian patronizers
of the Park, on such occasions, disappear from
your sight. They vanish almost instantaneously.
A few seconds ago, you saw from twenty to thirty
thousand, distributed over a space of three-
quarters of a mile in length, and all promenad-
ing the charming place in the utmost imaginable
security; now you see them suddenly take to
their heels; in a few seconds more, they have
all disappeared. You could hardly have supposed they could have more expeditiously made
themselves scarce, had they been spirited up
into the clouds by some mysterious agency.

It is not to be wondered at that a smart
shower, coming at an unexpected moment,
should be to those of both sexes who are fond

of decking their persons with "elegant attire,"
an object of special aversion; for a more ludicrous, if not pitiable spectacle, than a thoroughly
drenched dandy presents, could not be conceived.

Lord Brougham, in a recent number of the
Edinburgh Review, mentions, that happening,
on one occasion, at an early hour in the morning, to be going with the late Princess Charlotte
into her residence in Spring Gardens, he contrasted to her the then desolate appearance of
the open space at Charing Cross, with the scene
of teeming life it would present in a few hours
afterwards, should the princess be in a situation
to require any demonstration of the popular
attachment. I have often thought of the contrast between the appearance of Hyde Park, at
an early hour, in a morning of May or June,
and the scene it will present, without the inter-
position of any accidental cause, in the afternoon of the same day, provided the weather be
fine. In the morning, your eye may detect a solitary pedestrian or two, loitering about, or, it may
be, going to their day's work; but you might

just as soon expect to find a salamander, if there
be such an animal in existence, amidst the everlasting snows of Kamschatka, as to see a vehicle
of any description in the Park before breakfast-
time.   The fashionables, and every one who can
sport a phaeton, or. gig, are all in bed in the
morning; while no hackney-coach or cab, is
permitted to enter the Park, no matter though
the first nobleman or the highest functionary in
the land, constituted the " fare" at the time.

To appear in the Park, before one o'clock in
the afternoon, would be considered, in the fashionable world, as decidedly vulgar.   In the
vocabulary of the aristocratic circles, when a
titled personage takes an airing in the Park,
any time before three o'clock, it is called a
morning drive; and, so far as they themselves
are concerned, it is, no doubt, morning; for
though, by that time, the day of most other
people be more than half gone, theirs is only
just beginning.   The earlier risers among the
working classes in London, get up an hour or
two after the higher classes go to bed.

To be seen in the Park, at any hour of the

day, after "the season" is over, would be set
down as such a flagrant infringement of the
rules which regulate the movements of the
fashionables in the metropolis, as would almost
justify the acquaintances of the parties committing the transgression, in "cutting" them at
once. The circumstance would spread with an
electrical rapidity through the circle in which
the transgressors moved, and would be universally characterised as "shocking!" "horrible!"
and so forth, the parties employing such language
accompanying the terms with uplifted hands
and significant movements of the muscles of the
face. Young ladies, in the absence of balls and
marriages to write about, would make the circumstance the subject of pointed allusions in
their correspondence with their friends; and
thus, in a few days, the conduct of the violator
of aristocratic laws would be known, talked
about, and universally condemned, from one
extremity of the kingdom to the other.

So exceedingly partial are young misses in
the upper ranks of life, to "an airing in the
Park,"—for such is their favourite expression,—

that they often speak of that fashionable locality in the same way as they do of their lovers.   One young lady protests to her acquaintances—and she heaves a deep sigh as she makes the re-mark—that she is *dying* to be in the Park.   A second calls it " quite a dear of a Park ;" while a third, with a languishing look, and a pe-culiar emphasis of expression, characterises it as " *the* dear Park."

CHAPTER III.

TATTERSALL'S AND THE TURF.

Situation and description of Tattersall's— The Yard—The
Betting Room—History of Tattersall's—Sketch of Mr.
Tattersall—Horse Races—Their origin and history—New-
market Races — Doncaster Races — Ascot Races—Epsom
Races—Miscellaneous remarks—Settling day at Tattersall's
—Betting— Making a Book—General observations— The
evils of the Turf.

TATTERSALL's! Who has not heard of the
name? And yet how few can associate any
thing definite with it? It is true, that most
people have a faint notion that it has something
to do with horses; but beyond that their knowledge does not extend. In the ear of the
sportsman and of the votary of the turf, the very
sound of "Tattersall's" has a charm of which
none but themselves can have any idea. An illustrative chapter on "Tattersall's and the Turf,"

will, therefore, I am sure, prove highly interesting to the general reader.

Tattersall's is a large house on the right-hand side of Hyde Park Corner, as you enter London from Knightsbridge. It is a place which answers the double purpose of an auction-mart for horses, carriages, gigs, &c., and for all descriptions of betting on the result of the leading horse-races which take place; not to mention various other modes of gambling. To the betting feature of the establishment, I shall refer more particularly hereafter.

In going into Tattersall's, you pass down from Hyde Park Corner, about forty yards, and enter a narrow way, very mews-like in appearance, which you proceed along until you come to a folding door, on your right hand, of considerable dimensions. This door opens into the yard, as it is called, which is about sixty or seventy feet in length, and fifty in breadth, and which, on great days, is so densely populated by the admirers of horse-flesh and the votaries of the turf, that you can hardly find standing room. On ordinary occasions, its

chief tenants consist of a set of persons who
may be designated as a kind of hangers-on.
Some of them are grooms, who have lost or re-
linquished their situations, and at present have
nothing to do; very probably have become so
indolent in their habits, as that they would decline to do any thing were employment offered
them. Give them as much porter as they can
swill, and allow them to talk with each other
about horses, jockies, and other sporting matters, and depend on it they will never dream of
" bettering their condition." Others of the
groups who are to be seen in the yard at Tattersall's, are men who *were* sporting characters
in their day; but who having sported away all
their money, can no longer indulge in their
propensities for betting. Their appearance at
once tells you that they have seen more prosperous times. But even now, in their altered and
reduced circumstances, the ruling passion, an
affection for sporting matters, retains all its
pristine vigour. They lounge about the scene
of their former doings in the sporting world.
It may seem passing strange, but it is neverthe-

less true, that they derive gratification from the
circumstance of being thus suffered to remain
in the place in which they were ruined, and
in seeing the persons by whom their ruin was
effected. Among the other persons who haunt
the yard at Tattersall's, are a fair sprinkling of
broken-down shopkeepers, and bankrupt tradesmen, most of whom had either a partiality for
gambling on horse-races, or carried on a too
extensive intercourse with the bottle.

Immediately on entering the yard, towards
the left hand, you will, if you do not take care,
run against a small fruit-stand kept by a Jew.
It is quite a portable affair, and displays so little
of secure wooden architecture, that it is in momentary peril of being upset by a gust of wind.
Whether it be owing to a want of capital on
the part of the Israelitish proprietor of the
stand, or whether it be that he has adopted
the sound principle in political economy, of
regulating the supply by the demand, I cannot
tell; but the fact may be verified any day,
that the stock of commodities exhibited at any
one time is not only exceedingly limited as to

variety, but also as to quantity. In the pear
season, the stock of that palatable description
of fruit, very seldom exceeds from three to four
dozen; of walnuts the average weight may be
from two to three pounds, and of nuts, from three
to three-and-a-half. These are the only varieties
to be seen at one time. So long as the pears are
vendible—no matter whether they be eatable or
not—the Hebrew proprietor of the stall nobly
adheres to his resolution of having nothing to do
with the sale of apples. When the season of
the pears is over, then the apples, in about the
same quantities, are admitted to the honour of
a place on the stand. On ordinary occasions,
when the attendance is small, the business
done by this Jewish merchant is of course
limited; but no one who had not the evidence of
his own eyes to the fact, would believe what
quantities of his commodities he disposes of, at
other times, to the turfites who lounge about in
that locality. It is quite common to see persons
who have lost their little all, or perhaps more,
if that be not a contradiction, than their little
all; it is quite common to see such persons
purchasing pear after pear, or apple after apple,

in rapid succession, and munching them with
an expedition, which either indicates the desperate state of mind caused by numerous losses,
or an appetite of a most extraordinary voracity
for every thing in the shape of pears or apples.
Neither the nuts nor walnuts seem to go off
rapidly; the demand is usually very limited
for them.   The purchasers of the Jew's fruit, it
may be, are of opinion that they have got
nuts enough to crack in the losses they sustained at the last race on which they staked
their money.   When an unusual demand is
expected for either of the commodities, I have
generally observed that there is a Hebrew boy
who sits on the steps of a small stone erection in
the middle of the yard, surrounded by dirty
bags tolerably supplied with fruit, and that as
the remainders of the stock of the proprietor of
the stand get low, they are replenished from the
bags of this boy.   I have some notion that the
latter is a wholesale vendor of these commodities, and that he supplies the retail merchant
with them at wholesale prices.   I am not, however, it may be proper to say, particularly

wedded to this hypothesis; nor does it matter which way the fact lies, so long as the Jew is able to meet the demands of his customers of the turf, on terms which are profitable to himself and satisfactory to them.

There is a sort of piazza at the further part of the left side of the yard, which shelters from the rain a number of vehicles of all descriptions which are there constantly exposed for sale. From the farthest end of this piazza, there branches off to the left, a lengthened sort of lane, covered at the top, which is set apart for the same purpose. As many as sixty or seventy vehicles, from the splendid carriage down to the humble gig, are frequently to be seen in this place, all intended for sale. I have sometimes thought that if some of the carriages which are here, could write their autobiographies, we should have some strange disclosures made to us respecting the rise, progress, and downfal of the votaries of fashion. Where now are those to whom these carriages once belonged, and in which they lolled about in luxurious ease, never dreaming of what the end was to be? Some

are doubtless, after being reduced in circumstances, in their graves ; having, perhaps, died
of a broken heart. Others, it may be, are at
this moment living in poverty and exile. Worse
still—who knows but some of them may be the
inmates of a workhouse ?

On the right side of the yard there is also a
piazza, which, like the other, is eight or ten
feet in breadth, and which extends from the
entrance up to the corner where Mr. Tattersall
or Tat, as he is usually, in familiar language,
called, ascends his pulpit to "knock down"
horses. This is the space of ground on which
the horses which are put up to the hammer,
are usually exhibited to the gaze of bidders and
others, and where, if any one wishes to see a
particular animal trotted, he will find Mr.
Tattersall willing and ready to give the word of
command, to gratify his wishes. Along this
piazza, while the sale is going on, there is
always a crowd of persons ; some of whom, by
venturing too near when the animal is being
trotted, occasionally receive rather severe kicks.

On the right hand, on entering the yard, is

the counting-house.   In the front, in the right-
hand corner, is the spot in which Mr. Tattersall
places and mounts his rostrum, when about to
put some of the " fine animals " which fall into
his hands, to the hammer; and on the left is
the most important place of all, namely, the
betting-room, in which, as will be presently
seen, many thousands of families have been
ruined by the gambling habits of their repre-
sentatives, whether in the capacity of husbands,
fathers, or brothers.   This room, one would
suppose, to be a spacious and comfortable
apartment, it being, to all intents and purposes,
a place for gambling on a large scale; for every
body is aware that the gambling-houses in the
metropolis are all fitted up, not only in a comfortable, but most of them in a style of the
greatest splendour.   Not so in the case of the
betting-room at Tattersall's.   It is on the
ground-floor, and is a gloomy looking, imper-
fectly ventilated, confined apartment, without
a carpet, without any furniture worthy of the
name, without any thing, indeed, which could
impart to it an air of comfort.   And yet so

intent are the various persons who frequent it,
on their gambling pursuits, that they are seldom
heard to grumble at the want of comfortable
accommodation.   It is often crowded,—it is
always so on great days—with one of the most
motley assemblages of human beings ever
compressed into an equally limited space.
There the proud and, in other places, overbearing
nobleman is on a footing of perfect equality with
the clownish fishmonger who spends most of
those hours not devoted to business, in the tap-
room of some humble wine-vaults.   The foppish
young aristocrat, on the previous night the
glory of Almacks, the admired of all the lady
admirers in the brilliant assemblage who frequent that place,—may be seen, not only submitting to be unceremoniously jostled about by
a bevy of pork-butchers, who, as if actuated by
some unaccountable sympathy, are all forcing
their way to the door at once, but familiarly
conversing and betting with some rough un-
cultivated Smithfield drover.

There are, in short, in the betting-room at
Tattersall's, on all important occasions, every

variety of persons, from the high-titled refined aristocrat, down to the individuals whose callings in life are universally regarded as among the most disreputable which are known; and all, as just stated, are there on a footing of the most entire equality. Those who are for levelling all distinctions in society—who are the advocates of a social, if not a political republic— would enjoy a gratification of the first order, were they to spend an hour or two, on any of the great days, at Tattersall's. They could not wish a better practical exemplification of their principles than they would witness there.

It is right to mention, in thus adverting to the indiscriminate commingling together of peers and plebeians at Tattersall's, that of late years the personal attendance of noblemen has not been so great as it used to be. Many of our sporting peers appear at Tattersall's by proxy; that is to say, they appoint agents, whom they authorize to bet and to gamble for them.

The number of subscribers to Tattersall's is about three hundred. The subscription money

is moderate enough, being only one guinea a-
year.

The precise time when Tattersall's was instituted is not known, a circumstance which may
be accounted for from the fact, that like many
other celebrated establishments, it arose from
small beginnings. It is, however, pretty generally understood to have originated about eighty
or ninety years ago. Its founder was the grand-
father of the present Mr. Tattersall. He was
looked on as one of the most experienced men,
in all matters pertaining to horse-flesh, in the
kingdom. He commenced business simply as
an auctioneer in the horse and carriage line ;
and in that line soon obtained an extensive celebrity, as well as got into a most lucrative trade.
He also made a deal of money by the successful running of one of his race-horses called
Highflyer. Eventually he built an elegant
mansion, which, with the view of perpetuating
the memory of the animal through whose
achievements on the turf he had gained most
of the money expended on it, he called " Highflyer Hall." Mr. Tattersall afterwards became

a proprietor of the " Morning Post " newspaper, and derived a considerable yearly revenue from it. He also purchased the copyright of the " English Chronicle," but, whether it turned out a profitable speculation or otherwise, I am not able to say. Mr. Tattersall, at his death, left a handsome fortune, as well as the business, to his son. The latter also managed the establishment, with great success, for a long course of years. On his death, it fell into the hands of his son, the present Mr. Tattersall. Mr. Tattersall has a brother who has an interest in the business, but he is comparatively little known to the public. Nobody who ever saw Mr. Tattersall presiding in his rostrum during the sale of horses, can resist the conviction that Nature intended him for an auctioneer of those " noble animals." In the rostrum he is obviously in his proper sphere. He enters on his avocations with heart and soul. He has no ideas of happiness beyond the auction-yard. The very sight of the hammer, or rather of himself wielding the hammer, is to him an enjoyment of the first magnitude. His own voice, when

expatiating in terms of praise of any horse that
"*is* to be sold," has inexpressible charms to his
ear.   There is not a sound in the world that is
half so musical to him,—except it be the sound
of some voice whose proprietor is making a
" handsome bidding " for the animal in the
market.   Mr. Tattersall, though a man of few
words compared with the voluble school of auc-
tioneers who have Mr. George Robins as their
head, is a very adroit and successful knight of
the hammer.   He is dexterous in discovering
who among all who surround him are the
parties that really mean to buy, and to them in
succession he earnestly addresses himself.   His
very look, unaccompanied with a single word,
has, in innumerable cases, appealed so forcibly
to some bystander, as to draw out " another
guinea for the horse," even when the person
had fully resolved in his own mind not to
advance, on any earthly consideration, a single
sixpence more.   He holds in utter contempt
the bombastical and unintelligible diction of
Mr. George Robins: he not only deems it in
the most miserable taste, but he regards it as

a complete waste of time on the part of the auctioneer, and a positive insult to the persons assembled. Besides, he is convinced that by his own plain homely, but expressive style, he " fetches " a far better price for his " fine animals, " than he would by the most high-sounding clap-trap sentences that human inge-nuity could string together. He usually con-tents himself with mentioning the pedigree of the horse, praising him as one of the finest ever known; affecting to be quite shocked at the idea of selling-him at the price offered; assuring the company that it would be positively giving him away, which of course neither he nor the proprietor can afford to do; and regret-ting that he cannot bid himself.

When, however, he has any first-rate horses "entrusted to his care," especially if he see some noblemen or other parties around him, who are likely to " bite," he deviates from his usual course, and tries his hand at a little flattery of these persons, trusting to the potent effects of that commodity in procuring some better " bid-dings" for the animal. " There, my lords and

gentlemen," will Tat. exclaim in such cases;
" there's a chance for you. You'll never get
such a chance again. My lord duke, I know
your stud is unrivalled; but this beautiful, this
unrivalled mare would be an honour and an
ornament to it. Do you say three hundred and
fefty* guineas for her? Three hundred and fefty
guineas are bid: thank you, my lord duke, I
admire your taste. She possesses rare blood;
just only look at the symmetry of her form;
she is perfection itself. I could, but I will not,
dwell on her matchless beauties,—they are not
to be described. Only three hundred and fefty
guineas bid for her. My lord duke, she will be
yours if some one else does not——— Three
hundred and *sixty* guineas are bid for her. I
knew that she is too great a prize to be suffered
to escape at such a price. Really, my lord
duke, with your lordship's known skill and
taste in horse-flesh, I should be sorry if you
allowed such an opportunity of proving that
you possess this taste, to pass. Three hundred

---

* Tattersall invariably substitutes the " e" for the " i" in
pronouncing the words " fifty, thirty," and so forth.

and *eighty* guineas bid for her;—thank you
again, my lord duke; I'm sure you'll not repent your bargain. Does any one say more
for her? Three hundred and *ninety* guineas are
bid. You see, my lord duke, your admiration
of this beautiful and excellent mare is not
peculiar. She will, positively, adorn your lordship's stud, as she did that of royalty, when
she belonged to it. Who says the four hundred
guineas? She's just a-going. One moment
longer, and off she goes. Her action, my lord
duke, is beyond all praise; she has no vice;
she is a perfect paragon in every way you can
take her. I must knock her down, my lord
duke; but I would really be sorry to see you
lose so noble and charming a creature for
the sake of ten paltry guineas. Just say the
four hundred guineas and she's yours. Thank
you, my lord duke, for adopting my advice. I'm
sure you'll never repent your bargain. Going—
gone. She *is* yours, my lord duke."

Mr. Tattersall is a dark-looking man, with a
rather full face, wearing a reserved expression.
He is slightly under the middle size, rather

stoutishly made; and very lame. His age appears to be from fifty to about fifty-five. The number of horses he sometimes sells in one day is almost incredible. There are instances on record, in which the number has been as high as one hundred and eighty. Upwards of one hundred is quite a common occurrence, to say nothing of carriages, gigs, harness, &c. When the work in either way is heavy, he is assisted by his brother.

Mr. Tattersall has the reputation of being an excellent-hearted man. He is a great favourite with all who frequent his premises, or have occasion to do business with him. His brother, who is considerably younger, has a very gentlemanly appearance.

From Tattersall's and Mr. Tattersall himself, let us now proceed to the Turf, in the sense in which the word applies to horse-racing.

Horse-racing, as will be afterwards seen, is an amusement almost peculiar to Great Britain. In ancient Greece it seems to have obtained to a very great extent; for the Olympic Games appear to have principally consisted of horse-

racing; only that the animals, instead of running as in this country singly, with riders
on their backs, often contested the prize with
chariots at their heels. " Nimrod," the most
popular writer of the day, on all matters appertaining to the " Chase, the Road, and the Turf,"
says, that in some respects the Olympic racing
closely resembled our own. He adds, that the
Greeks " had their course for full-aged horses,
and their course for colts; and their prize for
which mares only started, corresponding with
our Epsom Oaks Stakes." In regard to the
riders of the horses, there was a great difference between the racing at the Olympic
Games and that which obtains at Newmarket,
Doncaster, Ascot, or Epsom. The proprietors
of the horses that contended for the prize, seem
in every case to have been themselves the
riders. At all events, it is certain that the
highest personages in Greece were in the habit
of riding at the Olympic races. Philip, king of
Macedon, and Hiero, king of Syracuse, were
among the royal jockeys of ancient Greece.
The latter was not only accustomed to ride on

these occasions, but on some occasions, we do not know whether frequently or not, won the prize. Pindar, as stated by the writer already referred to, mentions, in his first Olympic Ode, which is inscribed to the sovereign of Syracuse, the horse Phrenicus, as that which he rode when, on one occasion, he was the winner of the Olympic crown. There is another most important point of dissimilarity between the horse-racing of ancient Greece, and that which is now so common in this country; I allude to the circumstance of the entire absence of that gambling and other dishonest and unworthy practices, which are not only the disgrace of the English Turf, but which attach a deep stigma to the English character. The Greeks contended at these races for nothing but the honour of winning the prize.

Of the earlier history of the Turf in this country little is known. It is uncertain at what period horse-racing first became a recognized and favourite amusement in England. Neither is it known whether it was imported from any other country, or was of spontaneous growth.

The latter is, perhaps, the most probable supposition, as we have no reason to believe that horse-racing was one of the amusements of any of those nations which, at different times, conquered this country. It is certain that it could not have been borrowed from any of the neighbouring nations, no traces being perceptible of its ever having obtained among them. The general opinion of those who have thought on the subject is, not only that horse-races are the native production of the British soil, but that they have existed, though not so common as of late years, ever since a century or two after the Romans took possession of the country. Strutt, who devoted a great deal of attention to this subject, mentions, in his " Sports and Pastimes of England," that the first indication he was able to discover of horse-racing obtaining to any extent, was found in a work written in the reign of Henry the Second. From the frequent allusions made to the race-course, and the breeding of race-horses, in the days of Queen Elizabeth, there can be no question that the Turf was, in her reign, extensively patronised.

In James the First's time, horse-racing seems to have got more and more into vogue; for he was himself a great supporter of the Turf. It is generally supposed that he was the party who established the races at Enfield Chase, where the prize was a golden bell. It is certain that he warmly patronised, by his personal presence and otherwise, the leading races which previouly existed. Imagining that the Arabian horses were fleeter than those bred in England, he gave five hundred pounds * for an Arabian steed; but the animal was beaten with the greatest ease by our English horses.

Charles the First had also a marked partiality for horse-racing; but his reign was too troublesome to admit of his indulging to any great extent in his favourite amusement. It was in his reign, and chiefly under his own auspices, that the Turf was established in New-market—now so celebrated for its races and its horses.

In the intervening period between the death of Charles and the Restoration, the Turf expe-

* Equal at that time, perhaps, to £2,000 at present.

rienced a great decline. The Puritans strenu-
ously attacked horse-racing on the ground of
its being productive of a world of immorality;
and their attacks were not without effect.
These well-meaning men may in their own
minds have magnified the evils which sprang
from the Turf; but it would appear from the
concurrent testimony of writers, who lived at that
period, that it was a fruitful source of immorality.

At the Restoration, horse-racing again re-
vived, and being zealously patronised by the
monarch, it became a more favourite amusement
than it had ever been found before. Charles
was the first sovereign who gave plates from his
own private purse, to be run for at all the leading sporting places. At these races he entered
horses in his own name, and with the view of
obtaining the best cattle, he despatched his
master of the horse to Barbary, and other parts
of the East, with money to bring home the
best breeds that could be procured. James
the Second and William the Third continued
the royal plates, but were not by any means
active patrons of the races. In the reign of

E 2

Queen Anne, the passion for the Turf continued
to extend itself; and in the reigns of the first
two Georges it had become almost universal.
About a century ago it had reached such a
height that there was scarcely a village in the
country that could not boast, if it was a matter
for boasting, of its annual, if not more frequent,
horse-races.   Even the "New Sporting Magazine," a periodical which of necessity supports
the Turf,—even this periodical admits that the
extent to which horse-racing prevailed in England about one hundred years ago, was attended
with the most injurious results to society.
"So deeply rooted," says that journal, "was
the interest taken in it (racing) by all classes of
society, and so large a portion of the earnings
of the lower orders was risked on this their
favourite amusement, that it was deemed pru-
dent, by act of parliament, to put a stop to the
petty races which took place *in almost every
village,* and to the *dissipation consequent thereon.*"   I will not in this place, follow up this
admission of the social and moral evils produced
by horse-racing, as that is a point on which I

shall have something to say towards the conclusion of the chapter.

Up to this period, the value of the plates run
for, was, in the great majority of cases, exceedingly low, not on the average exceeding 15l.
The act referred to, namely, the 13th of George
the Second, prohibited all races where the
prize run for was under the value of 50l. This
had the effect of putting down a vast number
of the races which then obtained in the
country.

George the Third was of too retiring and
domesticated a turn to be an active patron of the
Turf. Still, as his predecessors for some gene-
rations before him had been in the habit of
giving certain prizes, he did not feel disposed
to withdraw them. George the Fourth again
was most enthusiastically fond of the Turf, as
he was indeed of gambling and gaiety of every
kind. Some of the horses bred by himself
were equal to any in the country, and repeatedly
carried off the Derby and the Oaks. His
brother, our late sovereign, was, on the other
hand, as averse as he was partial to the Turf.

Still, being one of the "good easy men" described by Shakspeare, he did violence to his own tastes by always appearing on the Royal Stand, on Ascot Heath, when the state of his health was such as to admit of his leaving the Castle.

The number of races of any note which are still kept up in England and Scotland, is about one hundred and twelve. Among these, the most important and most celebrated, are Newmarket, Doncaster, Ascot, and Epsom.

NEWMARKET, ever since its establishment in the reign of Charles the First, has maintained the ascendancy over all the others, though the palm of superiority has of late been disputed with it by the Epsom races of June. Prior to 1753 there were only two races in the year at Newmarket; now there are seven. In this respect Newmarket has a pre-eminence over every other race-course in England; for in no other instance are there more than two meetings in one year: in most cases there is only one. Formerly there were six and eight-mile races at Newmarket; now the greatest distance run is

four miles. Even this is a great deal too much.
It always more or less injures the horses;—
sometimes it kills them outright. To avoid the
latter evil, there is now an understanding among
the competitors and their jockeys, that in all
four-mile heats the horses will trot half the
distance. The race-course at Newmarket is
circular. The last meeting in the year continues for a week.

But as neither Newmarket nor Doncaster
can, properly speaking, be considered a legiti-
mate subject for a work which professes to treat
of the metropolis, I shall pass over the former
place without further observation, and after a
remark or two on the Doncaster races, come to
those held at Ascot and Epsom, as the vast
majority of persons who attend these races,
or bet on the results, reside in the modern
Babylon; and consequently render the illustra-
tion and discussion of racing at Ascot and
Epsom, a necessary part of my plan.

DONCASTER RACES were instituted upwards
of seventy years ago by Colonel St. Leger, a gentleman residing in the neighbourhood. They

soon acquired a celebrity and importance
equalled only by those of Newmarket, Ascot,
and Epsom. Of late years, however, the Doncaster races have been rapidly on the wane,
chiefly in consequence of the notoriously dishonest practices which have been committed at
the St. Leger by various gangs of unprincipled
gamblers from London. With the view of
lessening as far as possible the chance of
future frauds or tricks of any kind, the money
to be paid by those who mean to run for the
St. Leger, the great prize of the races, has
been raised, within the last few years, from
twenty-five to fifty sovereigns. When the
amount was twenty-five pounds, it was, to use
sporting phraseology, "pay or play;" that is,
that if the party did not choose to run his horse,
he should forfeit the whole of his money : now,
in the event of his voluntarily withdrawing his
horse, or any circumstance occurring to prevent
the animal's running, he only forfeits half of his
subscription, namely, twenty-five pounds. The
St. Leger prize is a large silver cup of the value
of four hundred and fifty guineas ; the winner

being entitled, in addition, to the whole of the amount subscribed, after deducting some necessary expenses. The amount received in money varies according to the number of horses that are entered for the contest. It is sometimes above 2000*l.* ; at other times it is under 1000*l.* The race-course at Doncaster is nearly two miles in length, and is of a semi-circular form. The races last four days ; Monday, Tuesday, Thursday, and Friday. Tuesday is the great day, the St. Leger being then run for. The Doncaster races take place about the middle of September. There is only one meeting in the course of the year.

Next come Ascot Races. Ascot is in the immediate vicinity of Windsor; and as the great race is for the gold cup given by the sovereign, all the arrangements are made by the Earl of Errol, Master of the Buckhounds, assisted by two of the stewards of the Jockey Club. These races are in a peculiar sense under the patronage of royalty. The sovereign, except when some circumstance of pressing urgency prevents it, always makes a

point of being present.   Even George IV., who
had so strong an aversion to making his appearance in public, scarcely ever omitted being
present at the Ascot races.   And such was the
anxiety of William IV. to give these races
whatever *eclat* they could derive from the patronage of royalty, that when, through physical
debility, he was himself unable to attend them,
he desired Queen Adelaide to honour them with
her presence.   The reader will, therefore, be
prepared for the information, that Ascot races
being thus so specially patronized by the sovereign, are better attended by the elite of fashionable society than any of the other races.   At
Epsom, as might indeed be expected from its
greater proximity to the metropolis, the numeri-
cal attendance is much larger; but, perhaps I
speak within limits when I say, that twice as
many of the higher classes are usually present at
Ascot races, as there are at those of Epsom.
Perhaps the largest and most brilliant assemblage ever present at Ascot races, was on the
day on which the gold cup, in 1824, was run
for.   I have heard it remarked, that it is doubt-

ful whether the number of the aristocracy that were present on that occasion, was not greater than the number that were absent, including both those who remained in town and those who were scattered throughout the three kingdoms; certain it is, that so much of the wealth, and rank, and fashion of England, has seldom been witnessed in any place.

As Ascot Heath is twenty-six miles distant from London; those who would insure good places on the stand, require to start at an early hour in the morning. Those who are later than seven o'clock have but a poor chance of seeing, or being seen to advantage. As early as four, you see magnificent equipages in, what an American would call, pretty considerable numbers, proceeding at a rattling rate along the road from Piccadilly to Hyde Park Corner. Gradually the number increases until six o'clock, when the road is crowded with them. You wonder where they can all have come from. You had no idea before, that there were so many magnificent equipages in London. You would be greatly surprised to see so large a number

of ladies out of their beds at so early an hour;
that being so marked a deviation from their
usual habits; you are doubly astonished that
they should muster in such numbers for the
purpose of witnessing a horse-race—a sport
which so peculiarly belongs to the lords of the
creation. Yet so it is; there is hardly a lady of
rank and fashion in the metropolis that does
not make a point of being present at Ascot
races. The unpleasantness of early rising, or
it may be, of not going to bed at all; the deafening din caused by carriages, horses, and pedestrians in particular parts of the road; the
danger of being half-broiled by the sun, and
half choked by dust; to say nothing of the
certainty of having their splendid dresses more
or less injured, either by clouds of dust or
showers of rain, or some other mischievous
agency; these are evils which are either suffered
with the patience of the martyr, or braved with
the fortitude of the true philosopher,—the empress
of fashion having decreed that the wives, and
daughters, and sisters of the aristocracy, should
appear at Ascot on that particular occasion.

TATTERSALL'S AND THE TURF.

The locality of Ascot races is one of peculiar
interest, both on account of the place itself and
the associations which are connected with it.
Not far from it is the noble forest of Windsor,
and Windsor Castle, which last has, for so
many years, been the favourite abode of the
sovereigns of England.   And in the vicinity of
Windsor were also the scenes of Falstaff's
amorous adventures with the " Merry Wives,"
the most popular, as it is perhaps the cleverest,
of Shakspeare's comedies; to say nothing of
the circumstance of Pope having so often resided there, and made its forest the theme of
some of his most beautiful poetry.   These are
attractions, however, which lose all their power
on a race-day.   The parties are not only too
fatigued by having risen at so early an hour in
the morning, but their minds are too much
engrossed with the events of the day, and their
attention too much distracted by the crowds of
people and equipages by which they are surrounded, to have any relish for such associations.

The race-course at Ascot is beautifully

situated. The scenery around is exceedingly
pleasant to the eye. It is a place, from a visit to
which the admirer of nature would derive no
ordinary pleasure at any time. Fancy then,
what it must be on a fine day, when the great
majority of the beauty and fashion of England
are present. A more dazzling sight is not to be
witnessed. How unlike the every-day world in
which one is obliged to live! From the excellent arrangements made by the Earl of
Errol, the brilliant assemblage not only enjoy
far greater comfort than is enjoyed by the vast
masses which attend Epsom, but the company
is seen to much greater advantage. Of the
additional charm imparted to the scene, by the
presence of the Sovereign, I need say nothing.
If the attraction of royalty was great under the
sway of a king, what must it be under that of
a virgin Queen, not yet out of her teens!
Those only who were present, can have any
idea of the eclat which the presence of her
Majesty conferred on the last Ascot races. It
was a positive luxury to see the easy and
affable manner with which she mingled in the

brilliant assemblage, and the condescending way in which she acknowledged the manifestations of affectionate regard which were made to her. There were thousands of ladies there, married and unmarried, who might have learned a lesson as to their own deportment, from the example of Queen Victoria. How strikingly did her unassuming, familiar, and inartificial manner contrast with the pompousness and *hauteur* of their demeanour!

Ascot races are of remote origin. They can be traced as far back as the commencement of the reign of Charles the Second; for it is proved beyond all doubt that he established races in the neighbourhood, out of which the Ascot races arose. Whether every intermediate sovereign, from his day to the present, patronised those races by their presence, as well as by their purse, is a point which I am unable to decide.

Ascot races last four days. They begin on the Tuesday of the second week of June, and end on the following Friday. The two great days are Tuesday and Thursday; and of

these two the last is the greatest.   That is the
day on which the Gold Cup given by the Sovereign is run for.

Though, for the reasons already mentioned,
the attendance at Ascot races is far inferior to
that at the Epsom races, the amount of betting
is not proportionably smaller.   This may be
accounted for from two circumstances.   The
first is, that the parties present being, in general,
much more opulent than those who attend at
Epsom, the bettings are in most cases a great
deal deeper.   The second circumstance which
accounts for the betting at Ascot being much
heavier in proportion to the number of parties
present than at Epsom, is that of many thousands of people betting on the result, though
they do not stir out of London.   They agree to
abide by the decision of the judge as given in
the public journals; and pay or receive their
money accordingly.

I now come to the EPSOM RACES, which
were instituted in 1779.   Lord Derby gave the
stakes which still go by the name of the Derby,
immediately on establishing the races.   On the

following year he instituted the Oaks race,
calling the prize by that name, because it was
the name of his country seat. It is curious
enough that his own horse Bridget won the
first Oaks. Epsom races take place only once
a-year. An attempt was made a few years since
to establish a race at Epsom in September,
but there being no prospect of succeeding, the
idea was abandoned.

Epsom races last four days. They take place
in June, commencing on Tuesday and ending
on Friday. Thursday, being the day of the
Derby, is the great, the important day, always
big with the fate of thousands of gamblers, some
on a large, some on a smaller scale. Friday is
the next greatest day in point of importance.
On that day the Oaks is run for, but the attendance on that day is not at all to be compared
with that which graces the contest for the
Derby. Still less important is the Oaks as
compared with the Derby, in regard to the
amount of betting on the result. Beyond the
mere circle of the confirmed and recognized
Turfites themselves, betting on the result of the

Oaks is scarcely known. What the extent of the betting on the Derby is, is a point to which I shall afterwards have occasion to refer. For a full fortnight before the Derby day, you hear of little else than the race that is to be run on that day. Among all classes of society, from the highest aristocrats down to the humblest mechanics in the metropolis, is the Derby the subject of conversation, and among all are bets laid, to a greater or less amount, according to the circumstances of the parties, on the issue of the contest. The morning of the day arrives, and for once in their lives the cockneys get out of bed before six o'clock in the morning. From four to ten, continued streams of persons in carriages, on horseback, and on foot, are seen pouring in the direction of Epsom. At so early an hour, as from four to five, you see nearly the whole of London in commotion, consequent on the determination of its population to be present at the races at Epsom. You see them hovering about you in every direction, previous to a regular start, all busily engaged in making the necessary preparations for the

contemplated journey. Some are loading their
coach, or phaeton, or gig, or other vehicle, with
those provisions which the cravings of their
appetites may render necessary before they
return home. Others are taking the precaution
of filling their vehicles with cloaks, Mackin-
toshes, umbrellas, and other et ceteras, in case
St. Swithin should take it into his head to give
them a little taste of what he can do in the way
of marring holiday enjoyments in the open air.
Others are anathematizing themselves and every
body else, because there is something wrong in
the harness of the cattle which are to drive
them to the race-course, or because some other
unexpected untoward incident occurs to dis-
concert their plans or delay their starting.   In
a word, there is no end to the diversity of circumstances in which the parties are placed
who are preparing to set out for Epsom. So
general is the bustle and motion around you,
that you can scarcely resist the conviction
that every body is out of bed, and that the
entire population of London are preparing for
a trip to the race-course. How striking the

contrast which the appearance of the streets
presents on the morning of the Derby, to what
it does on any other day, when you only see
here and there some lazy apprentice creeping
towards his employer's; or, it may be, some
solitary chimney-sweep, crawling along, with
brush in hand and soot-bags on his back.
And see the aspect of the various streets and
roads which lead to the great road which con-
ducts you to Epsom.   See the lines of carriages,
cabriolets, carts, and every conceivable vehicle;
the rows of horsemen, and the streams of pedestrians.   You are surprised at as well as gratified with the sight.   You ask yourself, where
can all the horses and vehicles, to say nothing
of the human beings you see before you,
have come from?   Do not press just yet for an
answer to the question.   Repeat it when you
have got into the great road, a mile or two
beyond Brixton, into which all the branch
roads have, like tributary streams to a vast
river, poured their respective complements of
men, women, horses, donkeys, dogs, and
vehicles of every kind.   When you have

fairly got out of town, you will have plenty
of time to ask yourself the question. Such
is the crowded state of the road, that you
will often have difficulty in forcing your way
onwards. Such a scene you never before witnessed; and you never dreamt that such a sight
was to be seen. You see nothing before or
behind you, but a vast promiscuous mass of
vehicles, horses, pedestrians, &c., all moving
in one direction. The scene has all the
appearance of a procession, except that it
wants regularity and arrangement. You already feel as if you were in a great measure
compensated for the unpleasantness of getting
out of bed at so early an hour, and for
any pecuniary sacrifice you may have made
to procure a horse or vehicle. And not the
least interesting feature in the scene, is the
motley character of the bipeds and quadrupeds
before you. The party in the splendid carriage
on your right hand, consists of two young noblemen and two dashing cyprians. In the go-cart
on your left are three Whitechapel butchers, in
the employ of Mr. Alderman Scales. Observe

the dandified aristocratic airs of the youthful
sprigs of nobility, and see the prudish demeanor and affected modesty of the couple of
"frail fair ones" who sit beside them. Then
contrast with this the blunt unceremonious,
"blow-me-tight" manner of the cattle-slayers in
the go-cart. They have no more polish, no more
refinement, no more affectation in their deportment, than had the half-dozen bullocks they
slaughtered on the previous day. Not less
marked is the contrast in the appearance of the
horses of the two parties. The steeds in the
aristocratic carriage, look quite as haughty and
as full of airs as their masters. They are the
high-mettled sort, and as if spurning the ordinary
speed, the driver finds it a difficult task to re-
strain them. They are just as pampered in
their own way as their masters, and a drive
down to Epsom is only diversion to them. Far
otherwise is it with the animal that drags the
vehicle which contains the trio of butchers. He
has all the appearance of a hard-worked horse.
The "shine is taken out of him." His head
hangs down, and his whole appearance indi-

cates that his spirits are broken by the conjoint agency of the whip and too much labour. If horses do soliloquise, there can be no question that he is congratulating himself on the crowded state of the road, which prevents his being driven at a more rapid pace. Take care you don't tread on the donkey with the little urchin on its back, which is immediately before you. Donkeys are proverbial for their reluctance to quicken their pace. This one is no exception to the rule.

" He is a donkey wot won't go,"

and, therefore, the little fellow who sits astride on his back, is as busy as he can be, in

" Walloping him, so, so, so."

You little rascal, don't be so cruel. What a pity some one does not seize the cane with which you beat the poor long-eared creature so hard, and apply it to your own shoulders! It would do one's heart good to witness the transfer. A taste of the "walloping" process applied to himself, would teach the young rogue to lay it on a little more leniently on the sides

of the unfortunate donkey. But where are
the officers of the Society for the Prevention of
Cruelty to Animals? Where are they? echoes
every humane bosom. They ought to muster
strong along the road to Epsom on Derby-day.
Do you see that country-looking man in a plain
gig, drawn by a still plainer horse? He is a
retired gentleman with 100,000*l.* You observe
that dashing mustachioed personage in his
handsome phaeton, with two beautiful greys?
he is not only a beggar in circumstances, but
was confined in the Queen's Bench prison so
late as last week. That is the Earl of ——,
two or three yards before you. He is an
inveterate gambler on the Turf, and has probably bets to the amount of 20,000*l.* depend-
ing on the result of the present Derby. You
see a poorly-clad pedestrian on the side of the
road about a yard from him: he is a jour-
neyman shoemaker, who, though unable to
muster the wherewith to pay for any convey-
ance down, has staked five shillings against
some other son of St. Crispin, on the issue of
the contest. You are struck with the diversity

you observe in the appearance of the crowds
who are wending their way to Epsom: far
greater is the difference which exists, could
we only perceive it in all its extent, in the circumstances of the parties. But I shall have
occasion to glance again at this topic when I
come to speak of the aspect of the assemblage
on the Downs* immediately before and after
the running of the leading races.

As every body, always excepting the inveterate gambler, who is bent on plundering as
many of his fellow-men as he possibly can,
thinks of nothing else; as every body but him
has left London for the purpose of enjoying a
holiday, you see nothing but smiling, con-
tented, happy faces around you. They have
by this time conquered the drowsiness and
want of spirit with which they had to contend—
owing to their rising at so unusually early an
hour—when setting out on their journey ; and
now they have all the appearance of persons
who are determined to be merry and comfort-

* The name by which the part where the races take place is
usually called.

able.   It is true, that many of them besides
the systematic gambler, have pretty considerable sums dependent on the issue of the races;
but somehow or other, they either forget all
pecuniary cares and anxieties for the moment,
or they all lay the flattering unction to their
souls, that they are to be gainers.   It never
occurs to them that some body must be a loser.
Oh, happy absence of thought!   It is only a
pity that the blessed delusion does not last a
little longer.

   Is the reader fond of contrasts?   See then
the altered aspect of the crowds who have
been to Epsom, as they return to town in
the evening.   You can hardly believe them the
same persons you saw proceeding to the Derby
in the morning.   Where is all their gaiety?
Where the loud laugh and the felicitous joke?
Where the liveliness of manner — where the
abundant flow of spirits?   They are all gone.
See how sad and dispirited, with comparatively
few exceptions, the streams of people seem.
Loss of money in many cases, and exhaustion
in others, have worked the change.   But I am

partly anticipating what will be said with greater propriety in an after part of the chapter.

Until twelve o'clock crowds continue to arrive on the race-course not only from London, but from all parts of the country within a circuit of twenty or thirty miles. What an immense concourse of human beings! There cannot be less than 250,000 persons there. And see how well dressed the vast majority of them are! Ragged coats or faded silks are but rarely witnessed. Whatever may be the condition of the pocket or the belly, there is no cause of complaint, with very few exceptions, on the score of the back. If there be a lack of money or of food, there is no lack of raiment. And how elegantly dressed are a very large proportion of the immense assemblage! The women are gorgeously so. You would find it a task of some difficulty to point out a score of ill dressed females within a moderate distance of the place at which you stand. Witness the forest of waving plumes of feathers. You wonder where they all came from; you had no idea before, that London could have furnished

such a supply.   How brilliant the aspect which
the vast numbers of ladies who are present
give to the immense assemblage!   Their attire
is elegance and splendour combined — their
persons are handsome—and the charm caused
by such a display of beauty and fashion would
be complete, but for the unpleasant fact ob-
truding on your mind, that a very considerable
portion of them are of exceptionable character.
But let that pass.   The face of the adjoining
hill, extensive as is the space it embraces, appears as if instinct with life.   Persons of all
ranks and classes are there crowded together
as densely as it is possible for them to be.
See also both sides of the race-course, fully a
mile and a half in length.   Carriages, coaches,
phaetons, cabs, carts ; vehicles of all sorts,
in short, are there ranged as closely as they
can be, three or four deep, from nearly one extremity of the course to the other.   And so
thickly tenanted are they, chiefly with elegantly attired ladies, that it is with difficulty
the parties can find standing room.

The people on the ground are so closely

wedged together along the margins of the course,
that one might as soon hope to make his way
through a stone erection, as to force through
them.   On the outside are donkeys without
number, some of them with and others without
carts, but all are there with the view of being
in some way or other, turned to profitable
account.   Many of them draw fruit, ginger-
bread, and other eatables to the stand; while
others carry the materials out of which stalls
of various kinds and for various purposes are
constructed.   The "show" party muster strong.
There is not a sight on earth you could wish to
see which you may not see here; or rather
which the showmen do not assure you is to be
seen.   Prodigies of nature are so numerous, that
one could have had no idea before, that she had
ever made so many, even had all been collected
from the time of Adam downwards, and from
all parts of the world.   As for legerdemain
tricks, there is literally no end to them.   The
conjurers do so much, and promise such a great
deal more, that one is surprised they cannot,
by some slight of hand expedient, convert the

stones or the grass under their feet into money,
and by thus enriching themselves at once, do
away with all future necessity of asking the
public to pay for their exhibitions. In the
theatrical world, great things are always done
at Epsom on the Derby day. Macbeth, or any
thing else you please, either in the tragic or
comic department of the drama, will be per-
formed before your wondering eyes, in about
five minutes' time. And see the actors and
the actresses; the scenes and the dresses! Did
any one ever witness any thing half so theatrical? I never did. Then see a great many
small tables, of very plain appearance, scattered
about you in all directions; and see those
tables surrounded by twelve or fifteen persons.
Don't these persons look very simple like?
Do you not fancy you see stupidity in their
countenances; they *are* very simple and stupid,
for they are playing at the game called thimble-
rigging, and the rogues who are the owners of
the tables are victimising them; in other words,
are cheating them of their money with astonishing expedition. Those large tents you see here

and there, and everywhere, are so many portable
hells or gambling places, in which the work of
plunder is going on at a fearful rate. Thousands are on the eve of ruin by the result of the
impending race; the ruin of the foolish persons
who are throwing the dice there, is already
proceeding at a most rapid pace.

The horses about to start appear on the field,
and the work of betting, as people see them
with their own eyes, begins afresh. In a few
minutes more, the bell rings to summon the
animals to the starting point and the starting
position. That moment there is a rush on the
part of the tens of thousands who were occupied
in amusing themselves in various ways outside,
towards the dense masses of men, women,
horses, vehicles, &c. which line the margins of
the course. A few minutes elapse between
the ringing of the bell and the issue of the race
being declared. And what an important frac-
tion of time is that to thousands who are present! Their prosperity or ruin—their future
happiness or misery in this world—their affluence
or beggary—the weal or the wretchedness of

their wives and children, are all wrapt up in the
events of five or six minutes.   Imagine then,
the corroding, the consuming anxiety of such
persons in the brief interval between the ringing
of the bell and the decision of the contest.   Oh,
the agonies of the suspense endured in those
few minutes!   The world affords but few instances of an equal amount of mental torment
being suffered in so limited a space.   See how
pale many a countenance suddenly turns.   See
the absorbed mind as indicated by the fixed
eye and unmeaning stare.   And were you near
enough you might almost hear, you might
certainly feel, the palpitations of the beating
heart.   The signal is given for starting.   "Go!"
shouts a loud voice at the starting post.   The
horses are all off.   Now commences the frightful tempest of conflicting feelings in the breasts
of multitudes before you.   The horse which a
party has backed against the field, starts fair;
he is a-head.   Imagine, he who can, the hope
and joy mingled with fear which agitate such
a person's bosom.   The animal is distanced by
some fleeter steed; the demon of despair seizes

the party in a moment, in his iron grasp. He
is a ruined man ; his wife and family are in one
moment hurled from the heights of affluence,
to the lowest depths of poverty.   He can
scarcely support himself; he would fall pros-
trate on the ground, but that he is kept up by the
pressure of the crowd.   Had he the means and
the opportunity, the probability is that he would,
in the agony of his remorse and despair, that
moment destroy himself.   This is no imaginary
picture—no exaggerated description of the tempest which rages in a man's bosom, when he has
been infatuated enough to stake his all on the
result of a horse-race, and that result has been
adverse.   It is only a few years since a case
was brought before the public which fully
equalled the one I have here supposed.   An
hon. gentleman, one belonging to a noble
family of distinction, and his own name well
known to all the fashionable world, not only
staked but lost on the Derby of the year to
which I allude, more by some thousands than
he was able to pay.   To such a state of excitement was his mind worked up before he knew

that the event was against him, that he was heard audibly, though nervously to utter—though the fact was unknown to himself—while the race was being run, "The D——* wins" —"The D—— wins!"—"The D—— wins!" The horse he had backed lost; he was a ruined man. He had not the means of committing suicide on the spot, and besides, the bustle around would have deterred him from the attempt; but on his return home, the very first act he did as soon as he retired to his own room, was to take a pistol and blow out his brains.

The moment the winner of the races is declared, the Stand, as it is called, is broken up, and the dense mass of people disperse themselves sufficiently to enjoy elbow-room. Portable dinners and lunches are now produced by all who were wise enough to provide themselves with such useful affairs before leaving town. Sandwiches are as plentiful as the blackberries of Falstaff. Thousands of persons, without being at all ceremonious, convey these tit-bits,

* Naming a particular horse.

with an expedition quick as thought, to their mouths, and not less promptly are they disposed of.   Here and there you see the wine or brandy bottle making its appearance, and without loss of time is it emptied of its contents.   Ladies who, at home or at parties, would blush to do more than take two or three sips of the liquid extracted from the grateful juice, now quaff a full glass, and it may be a second, with as much despatch, and as little ceremony, as would an officer of the Tenth Hussars.   Eating, in some shape or other, may be said to be everywhere the order of the day ;   for most of those who took no dinner with them, purchase a pennyworth of bread, biscuit, or ginger-bread.   In the shape of vendible liquids, there are sundry articles, severally baptized porter, gin, and ginger-beer.   If you have nothing drinkable of your own, you are glad to become purchasers ; for what between the heat of the weather, the dust that is flying about, and the extreme pressure of the crowd, from which you have just partly escaped, you feel as thirsty as if you could drink up the Thames at

one draught. Do you patronise the porter, the
gin, or the ginger-beer ?   No matter which ;
you will soon discover that they are all the same
in this one respect,—that the one-half, and the
largest half too, consists of water ; and as if to
aggravate the evil, there is strong reason to
suspect that it is not of the purest sort.   The
truth is, that the liquids vended at Epsom races
are like the razors immortalised by Peter Pindar
the younger—made to sell, not to drink.   The
poor wight who is doomed to drink either of
the ungrateful liquids, can scarcely help cursing
the hardness of his destiny, when he hears, in
the vehicle next to him, the bursting of a bottle
of delicious champagne, and sees glass after
glass transferred to some gentleman's or lady's
lips.   Our enjoyments are said to be heightened
by contrasting them with the privations of others ;
not less true is it that the magnitude of the evils
we are doomed to suffer is increased, when
we compare those evils with the good things
enjoyed by our neighbours.   Philosophers may
talk as they please about the excellence and
beauty of fortitude ; and moralists may tell us

that it is our duty to be content with our lot;
it is easy enough to preach up doctrines like
these : it is a very different, and rather difficult
matter to practise them under such circumstances as I am attempting to describe. I
should cheerfully perform a pilgrimage of some
distance to see the man without a drop of anything drinkable, while almost expiring of thirst,
and yet, without a murmur or the slightest feeling of dissatisfaction with his circumstances,
could see his next neighbour quaffing glass
after glass of the choicest champagne.

The ground is again all in a hubbub. Every
thing around seems instinct with human life
and motion. Your ears are almost rendered deaf
by the Babel of sounds which salute, or, rather,
grate upon them. Could you have before supposed that it was within the compass of possibility that any person however "gifted with the
gab," could have been so voluble, if not so
eloquent, in praise of his ginger-beer, as that
stentorian-voiced fellow who is bawling out the
pretended good qualities of his wash ? Hear
again, that unshaved ruffian-looking person

praising his ginger-bread to the skies. Don't
you wonder that that young rascal without
hat, cap, or napkin,—without anything indeed
worthy of the name of clothing, but with a face
which has clearly not come in contact with
water for the last eight days,—don't you wonder
that he is not quite hoarse if not speechless,
from the very excess of his oratorical efforts to
attract purchasers for his pies? To be sure, such
exertions would kill any one else, but these fellows are inured to the thing : it has become a
second nature to them ; a mere matter-of-course
affair.

The thimble-riggers are reaping a rich harvest
from the cockney greenhorns, who fancy that
they see the thimble which "kivers" the pea.
The thimble is lifted ; there is no pea there ; but
the money of the simpleton finds an immediate
passage to the pocket of the rogue who is playing at victims. Ah ! but though mistaken this
time, the greenhorn will not be so again. He
watches the rapid motions of the thimble-rigger;
he is quite certain where the pea is now.
" Half-a-crown !—a crown !—a sovereign !" as

the case may be, " that it's there !" pointing to a
particular thimble. It is lifted. Where is the pea?
Echo answers, Where ?   " It is not there any
how," observes a clownish-looking country lad
who is standing by, but has too much sense to
throw his money away.   "This beats every
thing ; this is passing strange," ejaculates the
victim.   Still he determines not to be " done:"
he tries again and again, and he is only " done "
the more.   At last his money is "done," and
therefore he must be "done" playing the game
of thimble-rigging.

Far more thriving still, because the stakes
are much deeper, is the business which the
blacklegs from London are driving within those
tented or portable hells which encounter your
eye in every direction.   See how rapidly the
foolish persons who are there risking their
sovereigns or five-pound notes, are plundered of
their money.   Scarcely more insane would be
the act of going out, throwing open their
pockets, and asking the first person they meet
with to empty them of the last shilling they
have, than is their conduct in going unto one

of these places for the purpose of playing with a
gang of rogues and robbers. The only difference between the two cases is, that in the first,
the process of cleaning out would be more expeditiously gone through than it is in the other.

The concluding race takes place. It is over!
and there is a universal rush towards the road
leading in the direction of home. Such a scene
of bustle and confusion as is now presented has
been but very rarely witnessed since the creation
of the world. Vehicles come in collision, and,
what is worse, pedestrians are often jammed between two or more of these vehicles. The
sufferers shriek, the ladies scream, and the
drivers of the vehicles swear at, and abuse,
and blame each other. Horses become restive;
legs are broken, and bones are fractured.
Great injury is done to the limbs of Her
Majesty's subjects: it is fortunate if no lives
be lost. The more tender-hearted of the myriads present feel for those who have already
suffered, and are filled with fear and trembling
lest other and still greater disasters should yet
occur. Eventually the ground appears less

densely peopled; the immense concourse assembled are now rapidly undergoing the process
of dispersion. The majority of the tenants of
the vehicles, and of the equestrians and pedestrians have now forced their way to the road,
and are earnestly bound in a homeward direction. Did you ever see such a road? Did
you ever before witness such extensive lines—all
as close as they can be, so as to be able to move—
of carriages, cabriolets, carts, horses and human
beings? Never, I will answer for it. You fear
there must yet be many accidents before they
all get home. Your fears are but too well
founded; for I believe there has never yet been
a Derby day in which there have not been a
greater or less number of accidents; many of
them serious: it is well if none prove fatal.

Has the day been dry? Well, then, such a
ludicrous spectacle as that presented by those
who have been to Epsom, on their return, was
never seen. Their throats, not even excepting
the throats of the most fashionable and delicate
ladies, are so many dust-holes on a small scale.
Their eyes are imbedded in dust; while their

carriages, cabriolets, horses, and their own persons, are all coated over with the same commodity.
They look, for all the world, like so many dusty
millers. What a figure do the ladies appear, with
the finery of which they were so proud in the
morning, and the preparation of which had cost
them so many anxious thoughts! Did it rain
heavily?—and Derby day is always remarkable
for being either very dry or very wet,—then it
is difficult to say which of the evils is the greatest.
A heavy shower at Epsom inspires the multitude with perfect horror. It plays fearful havoc
with the ladies' dresses, and gives the whole
assemblage the most crest-fallen and melancholy appearance which it were possible to
imagine. See how drenched and downcast
they look on their way home! One can hardly
persuade himself that these are the parties he
saw going to Epsom in the morning, so full of
life and gaiety in their countenances and demeanour. How sad are their visages now! They
are heartily sick of horse-racing; and their only
wonder is that they were silly enough to leave
their comfortable beds and their happy homes—

assuming them to be happy—in the morning, on such an errand as that on which they had gone. And yet after all, the chance is that they will go again next year should they be living and well, and have the necessary ways and means.*

Such is an attempted description of a Derby day at Epsom. It falls short of the actual thing itself. It is a scene which is not to be described. To form a correct idea of it, it must be witnessed.

Settling-day at Tattersall's, after the Derby, is always a day of great importance. It takes place on the Tuesday after the races. The room is crowded with sporting characters of all descriptions. With what opposite feelings,—in what different moods of mind do the parties

---

* I should here observe that the usual charge for a horse and gig to Epsom on the Derby day, is four guineas, being, as the sporting characters phrase it, a guinea for every horse-leg. If a coach and two horses be preferred, the charge is eight guineas; if a coach and four, sixteen. Coaches and six are out of the question; nobody thinks of hiring a vehicle with six horses. Very possibly one good reason for this, independently of the expense, is, that very few of our modern Corinthians could drive six in hand.

meet! The entire assemblage, and a motley
looking assemblage it is, in more respects than
one,—may be ranged into two classes: those
who have won, and those who have lost. A
physiognomist, of very ordinary skill in the art,
might easily enough tell to which of the two
classes almost every individual before him belongs. The unfortunate wight who has lost his
money is dull and downcast in his looks,—of
pale complexion,—hurried in his manner, and
is altogether quite crestfallen. If there be
an occasional smile observable in his countenance, you perceive at once it is not natural: it
is of forced production. It is got up for the occasion, in the vain hope that he will so far impose
on those around him, as to pass himself off for a
philosopher who can firmly, and with fortitude,
bear up under his adversities. But even if his
forced smiles were so far successful, his abrupt
and irritable manner of speaking would dispel the
delusion, and reveal the depth and bitterness
of his chagrin at his own folly. In the case of
many, you see the self-reproaches and regrets
which agitate their breasts as clearly exhibited

in the confusion and uneasiness of their manner, as if the fact that they had been losers had been written on their foreheads. Every thing around them is odious in their eyes. The very place is hateful to them : doubly so are those who have won their money, and who are now about to receive it. The Bank-of-England notes with which they meet their losses, formerly so pleasant to gaze on, are an abomination in their sight; or, if they pay with a cheque, or by bill, equally obnoxious is the " instrument of exchange." The winners, on the other hand, carry their good fortune in their faces. They are no knights of the woful countenance. See the contrast which the physiognomy of the winner presents to that of the loser ! Was there ever any thing more striking ? Who could believe that the human face was capable of such opposite expressions ? He whose speculations have been crowned with good fortune is the very incarnation of all that is cheerful and agreeable. He smiles within himself, and he smiles on every one and every thing around him. But you perceive a special proficiency in

the art of smiling as he looks on and converses
with the party at whose expense, very possibly
ruin, he has filled his pockets. He talks in
honied accents; he is " a bundle of sweets."
He appears so remarkably obliging, and so full
of the milk of human kindness, that you almost
begin to doubt whether Mr. Owen's pictures of
the excellence and amiability of human nature,
be over-coloured in the slightest degree. You
never, in other words, felt yourself before in so
suitable a condition for believing in the possibility
of a social millennium on earth. And then see
the eagerness with which he receives the money,
and the infinite delight with which he puts it
into his capacious pocket-book; an eagerness
and delight which are greatly heightened by
the reluctance with which the losing party
drags it from his coffers.

It is a painful reflection, that men can be
found—and most generally found, too, in the
upper and middling ranks of life—who could
thus take a pleasure in preying on each other.
The one's pain is the other's pleasure; the
one's sorrow is the other's joy ; the one's misery

is the other's happiness. The better or gambler
—for the latter is the most appropriate word—
coolly seeks to make his own fortune at the utter
ruin of another, and that other, most probably,
a friend.   He wishes to be rich by reducing the
other to beggary.   No truly noble mind could
consent to receive money on such conditions.
If there were no other argument against this
species of gambling than this one, it ought to put
an end to the practice at once, for it is utterly
destructive of all the better feelings of our
nature.

When a party who has lost, does not appear
at Tattersall's on settling-day, to discharge his
obligations, he is spoken of as one who does
not "show."   If he takes flight to the Conti-
nent or some other place, he is called a Le-
vanter.

The same term is made use of on the Stock
Exchange to characterise those who are unable or unwilling to pay the amount of their
losses.   I believe the term owes its origin to
the circumstance of some persons of distinction
at a former period, who quitted the country to

escape from their creditors, having sought a
place of refuge in the Levant.

On settling-day in Tattersall's, there are occasionally violent disputes between the winning
and the losing parties. The latter, as may well
be supposed, are always in that angry mood of
mind which predisposes the party to quarrel
with his fortunate opponent. If there be room
for a quibble,—any pretext for the non-payment
of the money lost, it is seized on with avidity,
and urged with the utmost pertinacity. Violent
altercations frequently ensue, and acquire such
a height as almost to frighten from their propriety the more strict and quietly disposed of
the sporting characters present. In several
memorable cases of late years, these violent
altercations have ended in blows. Who does
not remember the celebrated squabble five or
six years ago, between an M.P. and another
sporting character, ending in an assault committed by one of the *gentlemen* on the person
of the other.

Sad disappointments are often experienced
at Tattersall's on settling-day. Only fancy

the circumstance of the party who has lost
perhaps two or three thousand pounds coming
up to the person who had won the money of
him, and with a lugubrious countenance, and
the expression of as many regrets as there were
pounds in the amount lost, informing him that
he is unable to pay the money now, but, very
possibly hopes to be able to do so at some future
unmentioned and unmentionable period. How
deep must be the disappointment, how bitter
the mortification to one who had been fondly
flattering himself that he had only to open his
hand to receive some thousands, when he finds
that not one farthing is forthcoming. This is
an every-day occurrence. Among the Turfites
there is always a large proportion of desperate
characters—men who are as destitute of money
as they are of morals; and who bet to the
amount of thousands, when they have not a
sixpence in the world. But common as such
cases are, perhaps there is no authenticated
instance of the kind on record, which can be
compared to that in which a celebrated sporting character, whose name I need not mention,

was, a few years since, the unfortunate, though
he had previous to the settling-day imagined
himself to be the fortunate party. His winnings
amounted to little short of 3,000*l.* and he only
received 20*l.* out of the whole.   About the same
period—I am not indeed sure whether it was
not at the same races—another sporting character of great celebrity on the Turf, won 28,000*l.*
from various hands; and yet he only recovered
2,500*l.*

The " betting" at Tattersall's has of late
years been practically reduced to a sort of
science by the more experienced Turfites. Such
persons, by carefully attending to what are
called " the odds" from the period at which
horses begin to be entered for any particular
race, until that race " comes off," might make
a limited certain gain, varying in amount according to circumstances, were they to confine
their betting to the taking advantage of those
odds.

This, however, they seldom do; they usually
suffer themselves to be seduced into hazardous
speculations to a large amount, and conse-

quently often, in that way, lose more than they
gain in the other.

The subject of betting is very complicated.
I am afraid I shall have some difficulty in
making it intelligible to those who have paid
no previous attention to it.   This, at all events,
was the case with myself.   I shall try to make
the matter as plain as possible.   After the close
of one particular set of races, say the Epsom,
the Ascot, the Doncaster, or any other you
choose, horses begin to be entered for the corresponding races of the following year.   I shall
suppose, for the sake of simplifying the thing as
much as possible, that the Derby has just been
run for, and that the "settling" of the following Tuesday, is over.   A certain number of
colts are entered for the Derby of next year.
One of these, either in consequence of some
great racing feat which he has already achieved ;
or his particular breed ; his fine appearance ;
or some other cause, becomes the greatest or
first favourite.   Another horse from the same
or some other cause becomes the second favourite ; and so on with the   rious other horses

that are entered for the race. Betting begins
to take place on the result of next year's Derby.
Eight to one is freely accepted against the first
horse; ten to one against the second; fifteen to
one against the third; and twenty-five to one
against the fourth, and so on.

Possibly, by the arrival of the Derby day,
the first horse may have risen so much in
public favour, as that the odds against him
have dropped down from eight to one, to
five to one; or it may be that something has
transpired to his prejudice, which will cause
the betters to venture twelve to one against
him.

The second, third, or fourth horses may
either rise or fall in public estimation in the
same way. The betting in the case of any particular horse may thus be very different, either
for or against, at any one period compared with
what it is at another. The alterations which
thus take place in the supposed relative chances
which the various horses have of winning, are
called "the odds," before alluded to. Generally
speaking, experienced Turfites bet, in some

shape or other, on all the horses in the field.
But, perhaps, I ought, instead of attempting an
explanation of the mysteries of betting in my
own language, to quote a passage on the subject which is given by Nimrod, a gentleman
acknowledged on all hands to be exceedingly
conversant with all matters appertaining to the
Turf.

"The first object," says that pleasant writer,
"of the betting man, is to purchase cheaply
and to sell dearly, and next, to secure himself
by hedging, so that he cannot lose if he do not
win. This, however, it is evident, will not satisfy
him, and he seeks for an opportunity of making
himself a winner, without the chance of being a
loser; which is done by what is called betting
round.   For example, if twenty horses start in
a race, A bets 10 to 1 against each, he must
win 9, as he receives 19 and only pays 10;
namely, 10 to 1 to the winning horse. This, of
course, can be rarely done, because it might
not occur in a hundred years that all the horses
were at such equal odds. Nevertheless, it is
quite evident, that if, when a certain number of

horses start, *A* bets against all, taking care that he does not bet a higher sum against any one horse that may win than would be covered by his winnings by the others which lose, he must win. Let us then suppose *A* beginning to make his Derby book at the commencement of the new year. *B* bets him (about the usual odds) 20 to 1 against an outsider,* which *A* takes in hundreds; viz., 2000 to 100. The outsider improves, he comes out in the spring and wins a race, and the odds drop to 10 to 1. *A* bets 1000 to 100, and *against* him. He is now on velvet : he cannot lose and may win 1000. In fact, he has 1000*l.* in hand to play with, which the alteration of the odds has given him.

"But mark, he is only playing with it, he may never pocket it, so he acts thus. The outsider, we will call him Repealer, comes out again, wins another race, and the odds are only 5 to 1 against him. *A* bets 500 to 100 against him, and let us now see how he stands :—

—————

* A horse that is considered to have scarcely a chance of winning the prize.

If Repealer wins, *A* receives from *B*   £2000
He pays to *C*   .   .   .   £1000
   Ditto   to *D*   .   .   .   500
                         ———   1500

Balance in *A*'s favor by Repealer winning, 500

If Repealer loses, *A* receives from *C*   .   100
             Ditto   from *D*   .   100

                               200
A pays *B* £100 ·   .   .   .   Deduct   100

Balance in *A*'s favour by Repealer losing, £100

" But is there *no* contingency here ? Yes,
the colt might have died before *A* had hedged,
and then he must have paid his 100*l.*; but, on
the other hand, he would have been out of the
field, which might have been worth all the
money to him in his deeper speculations on other
horses. But let us suppose our colt to have
remained at the original odds, viz., 20 to 1. In
that case *A* must have betted 2000 to 100

against him, and then no harm would have arisen.

"In what is called making a book on a race, it is evident that the better must be early in the market, taking and betting the odds for and against each horse; for backing a favourite to run is not his system. His chief object is to take long odds against such horses as he fancies, and then await the turn of the market, when he sells dearly what he has purchased cheaply. For example, how often does it happen that 12 to 1 is the betting against a horse two months before his race, and before he starts it is only 4 to 1? If the better has 1200 to 100 against him, and then bets 400 to 100 the other way, he risks nothing, but has a chance to win 800*l.* It is by this system of betting that it often becomes a matter of indifference to a man which horse wins, his money being so divided amongst them all.   In fact, what is called an outsider is often the best winner for him, as in that case he pockets all the bets he has made against those horses which *gentlemen and their friends have fancied.*"

This extract from " Nimrod " will let the uninitiated reader in some measure into the secret
of betting on the result of horse-races ; but the
betting among experienced Turfites is usually
much more complicated and extensive in its ramifications than could be supposed from the above
explanatory observations.   It is, indeed, so
complicated that no description could convey a
correct idea of it.   To understand or master
its details thoroughly, it would be necessary
that the party should serve, if I may so speak,
an apprenticeship of some length in Tattersall's
and the ring.

Prior to betting heavily, it is of course customary to pay every possible attention to the
condition of the various horses entered for the
race ; and none but a Turfite can have any conception of the assiduous attention with which
every movement of a favourite horse is watched
from the time he is nominated for the race
until that race comes off.   Persons who have
access to the stable are often bribed with large
sums, by parties who are likely to be affected
to some extent by the way in which he runs, to

furnish such parties with all the information
they can respecting his health, his appearance,
the manner in which he eats his meat, and so
forth. Not half so intense is the general interest
felt in a popular sovereign, when that sovereign
is supposed to be in a dangerous state, as is the
interest felt by a Turfite in the condition of a
favourite horse, when the animal is supposed to
be, or actually is unwell. Regular bulletins of
the state of his health, duly attested by the sig-
nature of the veterinary surgeon in attendance,
are forwarded by the proprietor to such persons
as he is desirous should be acquainted with the
real state of matters. How such a horse takes
his medicine,—how he feels on the following
day,—how he looks,—how he eats, drinks, or
walks, are matters which are all most scrupu-
lously attended to, and are talked over with the
greatest seriousness by those who have betted
heavily in his favour. It is unnecessary to add,
that the greatest care is exercised in the treat-
ment of the horse by the party appointed to
train him up for the great field-day. The
animal is literally nursed by his trainer. His

meals are regulated with the most scrupulous
care, lest he should either not get enough, or
too much. Then he receives a certain amount
of exercise, that amount being at all times regulated by the varied circumstances which may
occur. In fine, not more solicitously or assiduously is the delicate member of an aristocratic
family, attended to by the nurse appointed to
wait on the party, than is the favourite race-
horse by his trainer.

It is generally by a knowledge of how the
various favourite horses are "doing" that the
Turfites regulate their betting. They carefully
weigh all the circumstances for and against the
various steeds, and then bet in favour of the
horse or horses that appear to them the most
likely to win.

The less experienced votaries of the Turf in
most cases regulate their movements by those
of the parties who are familiarly, though erro-
neously, characterised by the epithet of "knowing ones."*   They back particular horses

"A mistake prevails," says a gentleman who is intimately
conversant with the Turf, "among the uninitiated with respect to

against the field,—that is to say, all the other
animals entered to run, merely because they see

the term 'knowing ones.' For instance,—should the favourite
get beaten for the Derby, the universal cry is, ' the knowing
ones are done,' whereas it is precisely the reverse,—they
would have been done had he won.   It is the 'public,' that
is, the backers of favourites, who in this respect, are honored
with the title of knowing ones.   The really knowing man is
one who ' bets round,' in other words, ' makes a book ' on
the race.   His system is to lay out a definite sum against all
the horses in the betting, and the more the better.   Should
he be lucky enough to ' get round,' and at an average of 20 to
1 against 25 horses, he must win, and this is very frequently
the case.   To make it clear that the favourite is a bad horse
for the knowing ones, we will suppose that a race is about to
be run—that ten horses are in the betting, and that $W. B.$
has made a 1000$l.$ book on the following terms.   Specifying
the horses by the first ten letters in the alphabet, he will stand
thus at the commencement of the race —

1000 to 500	.	(2 to 1) .	against A
1000 to 333	.	(about 3 to 1) .	against B
1000 to 250	.	(4 to 1) .	against C
1000 to 167	.	(about 6 to 1) .	against D
1000 to 125	.	(8 to 1) .	against E
1000 to 100	.	(10 to 1) .	against F
1000 to 83	.	(about 12 to 1) .	against G
1000 to 70	.	(about 14 to 1) .	against H
1000 to 50	.	(20 to 1) .	against I
1000 to 40	.	(25 to 1) .	against J

" Now, it is obvious that the favourite, $A.$, is the worst horse

Turfites of distinguished reputation doing the
same.   This is often found to be "an egregious
error," as will be made sufficiently clear in
another part of the chapter.

With the mass of adventurers on the result of
any particular race, who know nothing of Tattersall's otherwise than by name, the standard by
which they regulate their bettings is the reports
in the public journals as to which of the horses
are the favourite.   They usually bet with one
another in conformity with the state of the odds
at Tattersall's, as given in the newspapers,
without possessing the slightest knowledge
as to what particular person backs this horse
or the other horse.

A considerable number of persons, again, reserve their bettings until they are actually on

in the race for *W. B.*; and should it win, he clears, after paying the 1000*l.*, only 218*l.* (this sum is made by casting up the
amounts won on the others—minus the 1000*l.* he has paid),
whereas, should the outsider, *J.*, win, he nets 678*l.* after paying the 1000*l.* to the backers of the successful horse.   Supposing that more than the ten ran, and that one of those not
mentioned came in first, *W. B.* would then win every one of
his bets,—the horses not mentioned being technically termed
his 'field.' "

the race-course, and have seen the various horses about to start for the prize. Every one fancies he is a judge of horse-flesh, and that he can single out the fleetest horse. And as it happens that most of those around him are of an opinion different from his, there is seldom any difficulty in finding a party to bet in the opposite way. A much larger amount of betting takes place in the field than most persons are aware of. I have heard of a case in which, a few seconds before the horses started, a gambling Whitechapel butcher, having accidentally met a nobleman with whom, through an extensive intercourse with him in matters pertaining to the Turf, he was on terms of as great familiarity as he ever was with any fellow-slaughterer of the horned creation,—I have heard of this Whitechapel butcher accosting his noble friend, with "Ah, is that you! I'll lay you 2000l. to 800l. you don't name the winner."

" Done," said his lordship. "Fearnought!"

" Will you double the money?"

" I don't mind though I do."

" Will you take a third 2000l. to 800l.?"

" Accepted."

" Go it again for the same amount?"

" No; the horses are off."

I do not mean to say that there are many such extensive transactions as this on the Turf, after the horses are in the field.   There are but comparatively few persons whose finances would admit of such deep play.   But I know that an immense number of such transactions, though to a less amount, take place on the race-courses at Epsom, Ascot, Doncaster, and other places.   Probably I do not over estimate the extent of such transactions, when I suppose them to be at Epsom, on the Derby day, little short of 100,000*l.*

The result of a race is often at variance with appearances at starting.   Horses which for the first eighty or a hundred yards would be deemed likely to be the last in coming in, are occasionally found to be the winners; while others, which for the same or even a greater distance are so far a-head of the others as to create a universal impression that they will carry off the prize, are found to be among the last to

reach the winning point.   Only fancy, in such a
case, how sudden must be the transition from
despair to hope—from sorrow to joy, which the
minds of those whose money is staked on the
horses first referred to, must undergo ; and how
suddenly on the other hand, the hopes and joys
of those who have betted in favour of the last
mentioned steeds, must give place to despair
and regret.   In the latter case the cup of good
fortune is raised to the lips merely to tantalize
the party ; for it is in a moment dashed on the
ground : in the former case the party drinks it
out before he is well aware of its being presented to him.   It is interesting to think how
equally matched, all circumstances considered,
the various horses that enter the field usually are.
Even in the case of the Queen's Plate races at
Newmarket, where the course is four miles, and
there are often ten or twelve horses contesting
the prize, there will not be a distance of
more than thirty or forty yards between the
first and last on reaching the end of the course
Two or three of the best horses are frequently
so equally matched, that after running the dis-

tance already mentioned, the judges have difficulty in awarding the prize. What is still more
surprising than the fact of their being abreast
on reaching the end of the course, is the circumstance of its often being a neck and neck
race between two or more horses from the
moment of starting until they have got to the
end of the distance. The most extraordinary instance of equal running, of which I ever remember to have heard, occurred a few years ago
at one of our leading county races. Three
heats or races were run at certain intervals of
time in one day, without the judge being able
to decide which of the two best horses were
entitled to the prize.

Just before entering the race-course the horses
that are about to run are exercised in a sort of
canter. Even at this late hour, innumerable
bets are laid on the event about to be decided.
Deep betting, however, as in the case of the
betting that takes place when the animals are
first exhibited, is seldom very general, being
chiefly limited to working-men, shopkeepers,
and others. The horses having thus " shown

off" in a small way immediately before entering
the course, every one naturally conceives himself
entitled to form his opinion as to which animal
is or is not to win the prize; and conceiving
this, he concludes, — and no one can question his perfect right to do so—that in this
free country he, as well as others, may back
his opinion by a sovereign, or crown, or other
sum, according to his circumstances. There is
one advantage which those who thus bet at the
last moment, and who lose their money, have over
those who have betted at an earlier period, and
that is, that they are spared the suspense, the
alternate hopes and fears, according as the
aspect which rumours, and inventions, and
actual facts assume, relative to the leading
horse,—which are so largely experienced by
those who had staked their money at a previous
period.

The amount of money which changes hands
immediately after the conclusion of the leading
races is immensely great. I have heard it
stated by one of the leading sportsmen of the
present day, that at least 1,000,000*l.* changes

hands by the result of the Derby race at Epsom. Surely there must be an exaggeration
here. If there were only half that sum, which
I am convinced there is, it would be a very large
amount. In some cases particular individuals
bet to the extent of 20,000*l.*, 30,000*l.*, and
even 40,000*l.* on a single event. In 1826,
Lord Kennedy, one of the most celebrated
Turfites of the present day, bet 30,000*l.* to 1000*l.*
against a horse called Crusader. In the same
year, another sporting character bet 20,000*l.*
against General, which was the favourite horse,
and won it, but it was commonly believed
there was foul play. Mr. Ridsdale, the distinguished Yorkshire sportsman, won at the
Derby race of 1832, the sum of 40,000*l.* by
backing St. Giles, which was his own horse,
exclusive of 2775*l.* in stakes. This was certainly good work for one day.

It is a curious fact, that a horse which easily
beat all the other competitors for a particular
prize, will sometimes, when running a race
which takes place a few months afterwards,
completely break down, and allow himself to be

distanced by other horses which were not supposed to have even the remotest chance with
him.   Instances have repeatedly occurred in
which the winner of the St. Leger, has a few
months afterwards, been beat by the very same
animals which he had left far behind him in
the first instance. This is accounted for from the
fact that some horses acquit themselves better
on a soft than on a hard course; while others
run better on hard than on soft ground.   Other
horses again may be unequalled at running on
a level ground; while anything in the shape of
an ascent proves fatal to their successful racing.
When a horse that won the last St. Leger, is
beat at the following Derby, or that won the
Derby, and is beat at the next St. Leger, the
losses as hinted in a previous part of the chapter,
are always enormous; such horse, provided
nothing has previously transpired to his prejudice, either through bad health, or otherwise,
being always backed to a very large amount.
It is unnecessary to say that the market value
of such a horse experiences an immediate and
serious fall.   There have been instances in

which horses, after winning some of the leading prizes, would have brought from 3500*l.* to 4000*l.* which would not fetch 300*l.* after being beat at the next great race. At the Epsom races of 1834, one horse, whose name I do not remember, was so great a favourite that 2500*l.* was offered and refused for him. He ran so badly, that in a few months afterwards the proprietor gladly sold him for 65*l.* Horses, on the other hand, that, contrary to the general expectation win some leading prize, rise as suddenly and to a proportionate extent in value. Fleur de Lis, for instance, was sold to Sir Mathew Ridley, soon after her appearance in 1825, for 100*l.*, but having distinguished herself by winning a number of prizes in the course of the next two years, she was then purchased by George the Fourth for 1500 guineas.

Horses of great reputation on the Turf always bring large sums. From 2500*l.* to 3500*l.* is quite a common price for a first-rate horse. As high as 5000 and even 6000 guineas, has repeatedly been given. One of the Bonds, the well-known proprietors of the great gambling house in Bennet Street, gave Mr. Beardsworth, 5000 guineas for Ludlow at the Doncaster races of 1832. Some years ago, the Duke of Cleveland gave 12,000*l.* for four horses.

So great is the supposed inequality of the horses that are entered to contest the leading prizes, that it is quite common to bet 50 or 60 to 1, against a particular horse. In several cases 100 to 1, have been bet that a certain horse would not win. The greatest disproportion I have heard of in the betting on any horse, was in the case of one which ran for the Derby some years ago, when 200 to 1 was bet against him.

While some horses never gain more than one prize, others have a continued course of good luck. The mare Fleur de Lis, already referred to, won ten out of eleven races. But the horse, which of all others, continued to run for the longest time, and which gained the greatest number of prizes, was Dr. Syntax. This horse continued on the Turf ten consecutive years, and ran in the course of that period no fewer than forty-nine times. Out of this number of contests, Dr. Syntax won the prize in twenty-six instances. Among the prizes thus gained were twenty gold cups.

There are many of the country races at which horses of all ages, and carrying all weights, are allowed to run; but at the Doncaster, Epsom, and other leading races, the horses must be of the same age and carry the same weight.* In the Derby, the competitors must be three-year-olds. Either colts or fillies of this age may run for the Derby; but for the Oaks none but fillies are allowed to start. The weight carried by the colts, in the Derby contest, is eight stone seven pounds; that carried by the fillies is eight stone two pounds. In the case of the Oaks, the age of the fillies is also three years, and the weight eight stone four pounds. But it is unnecessary to enter in detail into statements of this kind, every place having its own rules and

* Where the horses are equally matched, the carrying one or two pounds additional weight would be decisive of the race. Some years ago, a horse that won the race easily when carrying the same weight as the other competitors, lost it when the proprietor agreed that three pounds should be added to the weight.

regulations in such matters. To bring themselves within the proper weight, the jockeys are
often obliged to go through a starvation allow-
ance for a week or two previous to the day of
the races. I have heard of one, who by this
means reduced his weight to the extent of seven
pounds.

But the hope of gaining the prize is a
sufficiently powerful inducement to submit to
the privation of their usual meals; for it is the
invariable practice to present the rider of the
successful horse with a handsome douceur. In
the case of the leading races, it is seldom less
than 200*l*. or 300*l*. The highest reward ever
known to be given to a jockey for his good
riding was 1000*l*. This handsome gift was
made to James Robinson, a Scotchman, by his
master, also a Scotchman, for riding Matilda,
when that celebrated mare won the St. Leger
in 1827.

In the case of the Derby, the St. Leger, and
the other principal races, the horses intending
to contest the prize must be nominated when
they are only one year old. They may be named

either at London or Newmarket. The last day
of the July Newmarket races, is the last day for
the nomination of competitors for the prizes in
question.

All disputes which arise about matters directly
appertaining to the Turf, must be referred to the
decision of the stewards of the Jockey Club.
This is the only recognised tribunal in such
matters. Its decision is final: there is no
appeal from it. The Jockey Club consists of
upwards of sixty noblemen and gentlemen of
more or less standing in the sporting world.
The stewards are three in number. One retires
every year to make way for another, the retiring
steward having the right to name his successor.

In a week or so after a great race has been
run, the winning horse is honoured with the
appearance of his portrait and an account of
his pedigree in " Bell's Life in London." In a
month or two afterwards the same mark of distinction will be conferred on him, in a different
style of engraving, by the Old and New Sporting Magazines. " Bell's Life in London," I
may here obsreve, is the only recognised news-

paper organ of the Turf. Which of the two
magazines is the leading monthly organ, is a
point which I cannot determine. Each main-
tains that it is more approved and countenanced
by the most distinguished men on the Turf,
than the other. The rivalry between the two is
very great, and there is reason to believe that
both are sufferers by the competition. Twenty
years ago, the Old Sporting Magazine was an
excellent property, but it has been greatly
lessened in value by the conjoint operation of
unskilful management some years since, and the
spirit and vigour with which it has been opposed
by its young rival.

The number of horses that run for the prizes,
whether at Epsom, Ascot, Doncaster, or any
other place, varies according to circumstances;
but it will be found as a general rule, that the
number is proportioned to the comparative interest which the races excite. The greatest
number ever known to contest the Derby at
Epsom, was twenty-five. This was some years
ago, but I do not now remember the particular
year. Upwards of twenty horses have repeat-

edly run for the St. Leger at Doncaster. The
greatest number that ever took the field at the
latter place, was thirty. This was in 1825.
Twenty-seven have started on two occasions—
in 1820 and in 1826. The number of candi-
dates for the gold cup at Ascot which usually
take the field, is from four to seven.* For the
smaller prizes, the number of competitors is
less at all the races than for those of the first
class. For the Oaks at Epsom, the number
seldom exceeds fifteen, and is generally less.

The number of horses that are entered with
the declared intention of contesting the prizes
at the various races, is always much greater
than that which actually takes the field. It is
often six or seven times as great. The greatest

* The reason why the field at Ascot is so small compared
with the value of the prize, is that the competing horses carry
weight for age; so that moderate horses have no chance with
those of the first class. It would very much increase the interest
of this race if the conditions on which the Goodwood Cup is run
for were introduced, which conditions make it a handicap
race, an expression which implies that the weights put on the
horses are in proportion to their public running. There is,
however, this one departure from this rule, that horses that
have never run are always weighted heavily.

number that entered for the Derby was one
hundred and thirty-five. This was for the
Derby of the present year. The number that
ran was only twenty-three. The number that
entered for the Oaks, though great, was considerably less. For the St. Leger of 1829, a
period when the races were at the height of
their popularity, the number of horses that
entered was ninety-seven, though only nineteen
took the field. For four or five years past, these
races had been declining in the public favour,
and the number of actual performances, if not
of entries, had been correspondingly reduced;
but there is a re-action in this respect this year,
for the number of horses entered for the next
Derby is one hundred and fifty-two. It is possible,
however, that out of this large number not more
than from fifteen to twenty may take the field.

There are various causes which conspire to
prevent a horse which has been duly entered,
from running the intended race. The nomi-
nator may die before the appointed time arrives;
in which case, according to the rules which
regulate all matters appertaining to the Turf,

the horse is disqualified. Or any accident may, before the day of the race arrives, befal the animal, which either entirely disables him from running, or deprives him of any reasonable chance of winning.

Another reason for withdrawing the horse may be, that the proprietor is in arrears for previous transactions on the Turf. Or the proprietor, seeing other decidedly superior horses in the field, may come to the conclusion that his one has not the slightest chance of a successful competition. Lastly, to mention no other reasons for the withdrawal of horses that have entered for a particular race, the betting on those horses may wear such an aspect as that the proprietors may, either directly or indirectly, have sufficiently powerful reasons to prevent their wishing that their horses should win, and consequently to cause them to determine on their withdrawal. This, of course, can only be where there is roguery in the matter, which it will be seen is but too often the case, when I come to speak of the tricks of the Turf.

In numerous cases, those who *fancy* themselves " knowing ones " in horse-flesh, are at
fault in their calculations.   Their favourite,
instead of coming in first, or in other words
winning the prize, is perhaps six or seven
behind, which, in the language of the Turf, is
called being nowhere.   On the other hand,
" outsiders," which, as explained in a previous
part of the chapter, means horses that nobody
thought of, because it was supposed they had
not the remotest chance of winning, sometimes
are the successful competitors.   It is impossible
to describe the mortification experienced by
those who prided themselves on their supposed
superior knowledge of horse flesh, either when
the animal which was their favourite, thus falls
far behind, or when a horse they looked on as
not having a chance of coming in even fourth or
fifth, is the winner of the race.   In many cases
the parties feel more acutely the exhibition thus
made of their ignorance in sporting matters,
than they do the loss of their money.

The Turf is on the decline.   Every friend of
morality, and every one who wishes well to his

fellow-creatures, will rejoice at this. What are now the leading horse-races, but gambling transactions on an extensive scale? At what time gambling was first introduced on the Turf, I have not been able to ascertain, but it must have been at least nearly three centuries ago; it is distinctly mentioned as being to a certain extent prevalent in the reign of Elizabeth. In that reign George Earl of Cumberland, as is well known, almost ruined himself by his gambling propensities on the Turf. Towards the close of the seventeenth century, gambling at horse-races appears to have become so general, that Burton, the author of the "Anatomy of Melancholy," who flourished at that time, emphatically though quaintly said, "that many gentlemen by means of race-horses, *galloped* out of their fortunes." What would Burton have thought if he had foreseen the extent to which the vice of gambling on the Turf is carried in our day? Thousands are yearly ruined by it.

There is a numerous gang of sharpers and black-legs, who make the plunder of simple-

tons who bet on horse-racing, a part of their
daily schemes and daily roguery. Their plans
are secret, but they are deeply laid and are
carried out with a skill and artfulness which
render their success almost a matter of moral
certainty. And even where they are detected,
it is not, unhappily, until they have fleeced
their victims. What villanies have of late been
brought to light, which have been practised at
our leading horse-races? But in no instance
have they been discovered in sufficient time to
save the unsuspecting simpletons whose money
was at stake. And what care the unprincipled
"legs" for exposure, when it comes not until
after they have pocketed the money of their
victims? Nothing at all; for they have no character to lose. And they know the law cannot
reach them. Who does not remember the dis-
graceful transactions which took place at the
Doncaster races of 1832? And are not certain
transactions of the most unprincipled kind,
which occurred at a celebrated race a few
months ago, and by which thousands have
been ruined,—still the subject of animated and

indignant remark in all the sporting circles?
The affair of the horse Ludlow, is still fresh in
the recollection of all patrons of the Turf; and
that of Harkaway at a very recent race, is not
likely to cease to be spoken about for some
time to come. Is it not beyond all question,
that horses, which otherwise would have won,
are often prevented from winning by the most
consummate roguery? In some cases they are
drugged so as to make them sick; in others
the jockeys are bribed to ride them in such a
way as to prevent their coming in first. A very
common expedient resorted to by the "leg" fraternity, when they have made their arrangements to their entire satisfaction beforehand,
is to withdraw the horse which was the greatest
favourite, by either purchasing him from the
proprietor or pretending to have purchased him.
In fact there is no end to the tricks of the Turf.
The ramifications of the roguery practised by
the mendacious gamblers who are so largely
mixed up with all Turf transactions, are so varied
and extensive, that no calculation or fore-
sight can guard against their effects. So cun-

ningly and skilfully are their schemes for plundering her Majesty's subjects laid, that they
often, with the view of gulling the public, bet
to a certain extent in favour of the favourite
horse, though they know he will lose. A little
loss in this way is amply made up by secretly
betting to a large amount the other way;
or by some other private arrangement made
among themselves. Another favourite expedient on the race-course is to invent all sorts of
rumours respecting different horses,—rumours
relative to the probability or otherwise of particular animals running; and thus raising the
odds, or causing them to fall in particular cases,
according as their own interests are affected.
Scarcely less notorious for the invention of
false rumours on the part of a gang of black
legs, is the race-course, than is the Stock Exchange itself. With regard again to the running of favourite horses, it is now so common a
practice for the parties interested to manage
matters in such a way as that they shall not
win,—that it has of late become customary with
the recently initiated, before betting for or

against any favourite horse, to do every thing he can to ascertain whether or not it really be meant or intended by the proprietor that the horse shall win.

The public, who know little or nothing of the tricks of the Turf, never contemplate the possibility of any person entering a favourite horse, far less of his starting him for the race, without being most desirous that he should win; and, consequently, are victimized without perhaps ever suspecting that there was aught else than perfect fairness in the matter. It is well known that many hundreds of pounds have been given to proprietors of favourite horses, to bribe them not to win the race; and it is equally well known that the jockeys destined to ride such horses, have when not directly bribed by the "legs" to lose the race, often received through the proprietors two or three hundred pounds for riding in such a way as to cause the horse to make a respectable appearance on the race-course, and thus lull suspicion of any treachery without winning the prize.

When I mention that a number of Jewish

black-legs,-- for the Turf swarms with rogues of
the Hebrew persuasion,—have severally, perhaps, betted from 10,000*l.* to 15,000*l.* that a
particular horse shall not win, and when I add,
that these are all leagued together for the purpose of plundering simpletons of their money, it
will at once be seen to be natural that they
should unite together, through the medium of
one of their number, in offering the proprietor
of a horse, where that proprietor is supposed to
be accessible to bribery, such a sum as will
cause him to guarantee that the horse shall not
win the race.

In innumerable cases, in which the proprietors were men of too much honour and
honesty to be parties to any such fraud, the
leading men among the "leg" fraternity have,
through the intervention of some person on
whom they could depend, attempted to bribe
the individual entrusted with the training of the
particular horse, to give him a particular pill the
night before the race, so as to make him sick; and
when this has failed, the inducement of some
hundred pounds not to win, has been held out to

the jockey booked to ride the animal. And where all efforts of the kind have failed, a sum twice the value of the horse has repeatedly been offered for him immediately before the races.

The late Mr. Mostyn was offered the unprecedented sum of seven thousand guineas, a few years since, for a horse of his which was the favourite for the St. Leger; but knowing that the offer was made for the purpose of enabling the parties to practise a fraud on the public, he, like an honourable man, scorned to accept it, though the probability was he would have taken a third of the sum after the races were over. Had the swindling brotherhood got the horse, they would of course have withdrawn him from the field,—all the parties who had betted that he would win, being in that case equally losers as if he had contested the prize but been unsuccessful.

The trickery which is practised on the Turf may be inferred from the character of the persons who most largely patronize it. Who are these? Notoriously the leading proprietors of gambling-houses in London, and the princi-

pal frequenters of those houses. Who ever
heard of a race of any note, without seeing
Crockford standing on the course, with his
hands in his pockets, and looking like one
whose mind is occupied with some abstruse calculations as to the way in which the impending
" events" are likely to come off? And see
how the trio of Bonds, the next greatest gam-
bling-house proprietors in the metropolis, dash
about in their splendid equipages. As to gambling noblemen and gentlemen : why there is not
one of any notoriety in our London hells, that
is not equally well known on the Turf. I could
here run over in dozens the names of dukes, of
marquises, of earls, and of noblemen and gentlemen of every rank, professed devotees of gambling at the hazard-tables of the hells in town,
who are equally notorious for their patronage
of the Turf. And how many of these are there,
who are bankrupt in fortune as well as
character?

Then there are the false notions of honour
that prevail on the Turf. Such are these notions,
that Turfites feel bound to pay, provided they

can at all raise the amount, any losses they
may incur by betting, even though their tradesmen and families should not only be suffering
the greatest privations in consequence of the
non-payment of the amount due to them, but
should be brought to the verge of ruin on
that account. How many poor tradesmen
suffered, and how many of themselves or their
successors still suffer, from the non-payment by
the late Duke of York, of the debts he con-
tracted with them ! And yet he always made a
point of paying the losses he sustained on the
Turf. It was the same in the case of his brother,
George the Fourth, when Prince of Wales ; and
it is the same with numbers of noblemen whose
names might be mentioned. Such is the morality
which obtains on the Turf! Such are the notions
of honor that are entertained by its votaries !

The Turf, then, is a most prolific source of
social evil. I am convinced it would be impossible to estimate the amount of mischief it has
done to morals, to families, and to society. It
first destroys all the better feelings of one's
nature, and then destroys one's fortune. Could

all those that are still alive who have been
ruined by the Turf, be brought into one place,
what a vast and wretched assemblage of human
beings would they present! The victims of the
Turf! Why their name is legion!

It is deeply to be regretted that when the results of betting on horse-races are so disastrous,
those races should be specially patronised by
the Queen. Of course, the blame does not
attach to her. The subject is one which, in all
probability, has never been brought under her
consideration. She subscribes to the Ascot
Races, and patronises those races by her presence, because her predecessors have done the
same before her. But it is to be regretted that
there should not be those around her throne,
who would point out to her the frightful evils
which are necessarily associated with the Turf,
and suggest to her that she ought not to become
the patroness either by her purse or her presence—especially not by both—of a pastime
which is productive of so much immorality and
of so much misery to individuals and families.
I am sure, that were a Sovereign possessed of

such amiable feelings as is Victoria, and who is
so exceedingly anxious to promote the cause of
morals, and to increase the happiness of mankind,—only aware of the deplorable and destructive consequences of horse-racing, she
would at once withdraw her patronage from
that pastime.

CHAPTER IV.

DOWNING STREET.

Its situation and appearance—The Premier's Office; Lord Melbourne, the Duke of Wellington, and Earl Grey—Chancellor of the Exchequer's Office ; Mr. Spring Rice, Sir Robert Peel, and Lord Althorp—The Colonial Office and Lord Glenelg—The Foreign Office and Lord Palmerston— Ludicrous interviews with Ministers—Economy in Downing Street.

DOWNING STREET! What subject could be so interesting? What street, amidst the thousands of streets in this metropolis, possesses a tithe of the importance which attaches to it? Most momentous to the British empire, and not to it only, but to the whole civilized world, are the daily doings in Downing Street. The well-being of the human race is often more or less affected

by the decisions which are come to there. But
of this, more anon.

Where is Downing Street? in what part of
London is it situated? the country reader will
inquire. So will the visiter to the metropolis,
whose stay is limited, and who is anxious to
see every locality possessed of particular interest.
Downing Street is situated in the heart of London. It is about a quarter of a mile south of
Charing Cross, and about an equal distance
north of Westminster Abbey, the courts of
law, and the houses of Parliament. It is on the
right hand, at the furthest end of Whitehall,
just as you enter Parliament Street. Every
one fancies that as it is the place where the
leading government offices are situated, it must
be a very imposing street; a place which will
dazzle the eye by its splendour. He finds
himself sadly mistaken when it meets his gaze.
He can hardly persuade himself that he has
been directed to the right place. He sees
clearly enough, from a little board on the
corner-house, that this is *a* Downing Street;
but he will not be convinced that it is *the*

Downing Street. It is so, nevertheless. And a miserable looking place it assuredly is for the most important business of the country to be transacted in. The street is short and for the most part narrow. Its length, I should think does not exceed fifty yards, and its breadth, with the exception of a small space at the further end, which has the appearance of a Lilliputian square, cannot, I should fancy, be more than eight or nine yards. The first house on the right hand side, on entering the street, is a very handsome building : it is the place in which the Privy Council hold their delibera- tions. But see the contrast which the houses on the opposite or left-hand side exhibit to it. The corner one is a public house, or as the sign-board outside characterizes it, a "wine vaults." The next eight houses are chiefly tenanted by people who live by letting out lodgings; furnished or unfurnished, as the case may be. And what dingy smoked-looking buildings do they appear! Quite in keeping with their appearance in this respect, is their dilapidated aspect. They are evidently of great

antiquity, and look so very ruinous, that the
wonder is how any one can sleep in them,
or cross their threshold without being appre-
hensive of their falling about his ears before he
awakes, or before he gets outside again. The
panes of glass in many of the windows are
shattered; in some they have been so tinkered or
patched, that it would require a little time and
no small measure of discernment, to say which
is the fragment that still remains, if any do
remain, of the original pane. A slip of paper in
some instances is substituted for glass; in
other cases a piece of old clothes is forced into
some perforation in the panes, for the purpose
of keeping out the wind and the rain. Then witness the parties who are to be seen at the windows. There are lots of children with dirty faces,
and very indifferent clothes; and the grown-up
personages, in some cases, though not in all, are
but little better. Would any one believe it,
that nearly opposite the last of these nine
houses is the official residence of the Prime
Minister! If Lord Melbourne be fond of such
amusement, he has only to look any day out of

his windows, to see little unwashed cherubs in abundance, on the opposite side.

The public house in the corner is one with which many curious circumstances are associated. It is the favourite place of resort of aristocratic coachmen and other male servants in the habit of attending on the great ones of the earth. And most amusing is it to see them there in the evening, smoking their pipes and swilling their porter, and to hear the familiar terms in which they speak of their noble masters. No one ever yet heard any of these Jehus, grooms, and so forth, adventure a difference of opinion from their masters on political questions ; but nothing could exceed the terms of familiarity in which they speak of them. They are " old boys," "jolly old fellows," " rum 'uns," " good 'uns," " chaps," and so on.

But it is due to the liveried servants of the aristocracy, who patronise the wine-vaults in the corner of Downing Street, to say, that while they themselves speak in terms of the greatest familiarity—a familiarity verging on ridicule— of their masters, they will not tolerate any one else, were he to attempt to do so. The coachee, who but a moment before was speaking of his noble master, Lord So-and-So, as an "old buffer," or a "reg'lar rum 'un," will not hesitate an instant to knock down the mechanic or other person who ventures to speak disrespectfully of him. More than this, there is not a jarvey or lacquey among them that will not resent with spirit any attack which may be made upon the nobility, as a class, by any Radical or other person, who has a dislike to the aristocracy. Earl Grey once declared his determination to stand by his order : if he wishes for allies in the business, he will find them in abundance in the public-house at the corner of the street in which, when Prime Minister, he resided for several years. Though not *of* the order, these persons are most devotedly attached *to* the order.

Every day—almost indeed every hour—pots of foaming heavy wet are to be seen, being carried up from the corner house, to the various offices in Downing Street. Who could witness this without wondering in his own mind for whom

are these copious draughts of Whitbread and
Co's. Entire intended.   Ill-natured people, disposed to have their joke, would mention the
names of persons high in office.   I think I may
safely venture to say, that this heavy wet is invariably intercepted by the porters in the halls
of the different offices, when the tour it makes
is extended beyond the limits of the nine houses
I have already attended to.

Many are the hundreds of letters; in some
cases stating grievances, real or imaginary, and
imploring redress; in others, applying for situations,—which have been addressed to the different members of the government from the par-
lour, aye, and from the tap-room, too, of the
corner public-house. The most curious instance
of this kind which has come to my knowledge,
was that of a person who daily, from this wine-
vaults, for several months, besieged the Duke
of Wellington, when he was in office in 1829,
with applications for some situation under
government.   The Duke's secretary became
quite tired of returning answers to the applicant's epistles, and the Duke himself of hearing

the fact stated every day, that a fresh letter had been received. The party was peremptorily requested to desist from troubling the Duke with fruitless applications : still he persevered. At length the Duke, wearied, like the man in the Evangelists, with the importunity of his correspondent, took up his letter and went with it himself into the Colonial Office, when, handing it to the Colonial Secretary, he begged the latter to give the party applying some inferior appointment in the colonies, in order that he might be sent out of the country, and by that means spare him (the Duke) any further persecution. It was done as the Duke desired, and the party still, for anything I know to the contrary, holds the same government situation in one of our colonies. *

The first house on the right-hand side of

---

* No more colonial nor other appointments will be got in consequence of any letters written from the public-house at the corner of Downing-street ; for while these sheets are passing through the press, that house, and the other eight houses already alluded to, are ordered to be taken down. The wonder is, how such a nuisance as these houses have for years been, should have been tolerated so long.

Downing Street, after passing the Privy Council
room and a passage which leads into St.
James's Park, is the official residence and
offices of the PRIME MINISTER. It has a very
plain, unimposing appearance outside. The
windows are small, and the height is only three
stories.

But, though it has but a humble unattractive
aspect externally, it is very comfortable inside,
being abundantly and splendidly furnished, while
the apartments, if not remarkable for their spa-
ciousness, are laid out with much judgment.
The rooms are about sixty in number, and extend as far back as the park. The house is
celebrated for possessing one thing, which, let
philosophers laugh at it as they please, is very
indispensable to human happiness: I allude to
its having what is generally allowed to be
the finest kitchen in the world. The only two
things requisite to extract enjoyment from the
kitchen, is to have a good cook, and plenty of
materials to afford sufficient scope for that cook's
culinary skill. The latter, namely, the materials are, I need hardly say, never wanting in a

prime minister's house, and the other, viz., a good cook, is an article which may also be easily procured, if persons will but pay a proper price and go to the proper market. I make this remark by way of preface to the statement of two facts: first, that the Duke of Wellington, who, though by no means an epicure, yet desirous that whatever he does eat should be prepared in the best style, has always taken special care that his cook should be a man of first-rate acquirements in the culinary science; and, second, which is the point I have specially in my eye, that when he resided in this house, during the time he was at the head of the government, he had in his employ as cook, the very person, a Frenchman of course, though I forget his name, who was principal cook to Buonaparte twenty years previously.

And since thus incidentally mentioning the name of the Duke of Wellington, let me add, that when in power, a person more close or attentive to the duties of his office, never crossed the threshold of any of the houses in Downing Street. Declining the innumerable invitations he was hourly receiving to dinner and other parties, in the mansions of the aristocracy, and resisting all the temptations to pleasures of other kinds, to which an individual of his station is exposed, he applied himself to the discharge of his official duties, with an assiduity, and zeal, and patience, which the most fagging attorney never exceeded, and which would have covered with blushes and confusion of face, thousands of our London clerks who are in the habit of complaining of their close confinement to the duties of their situations.

Earl Grey also lived constantly in the official residence in Downing Street, when he presided over the destinies of our empire; but though, on the whole, attentive to the duties of his office, he was not so laborious and indefatigable in the discharge of those duties as his predecessor the Duke of Wellington.

As for Lord Melbourne, again, he has never formally taken up his residence in Downing Street. He will not, to use a familiar phrase, "move a step" on any account from South Street. Why he so tenaciously clings to the one residence, and so systematically shuns the other, is a problem the solution of which I leave to others. He is, as I hinted in a previous work,* the most light-hearted prime minister that ever presided at the helm of public affairs. I should like to see the political event, short of his ejection from office, that would give him a moment's concern. I will answer for it, that he did not lose his usual afternoon's nap on the day on which he received the intelligence of Earl Durham's resignation of the Governor-General-ship of Canada. No one ever yet perceived a thoughtful expression on his countenance, caused by the pressure of national affairs. He is still the same laughter-loving, jolly-looking person he was before his elevation to office. I will undertake to assert, that he is the most easy-minded man in the country. He takes care not to hurt himself by over-exertion in the discharge of the duties of the premiership. He has no notion of doing anything which may be left undone : it were well if he did not some-

* The Second Series of "Random Recollections of the Lords and Commons."

times leave undone the things which he ought
to have done.   Neither will he put himself to
the trouble of doing, in his own person, what
can be done by proxy.   He laughs at the idea
of men in office over-working themselves in the
public service ; and is determined, that no consideration on earth shall induce him to become
a living martyr for his country, by submitting
to "too much" of the drudgery of office.   In
conformity with this principle, he is not to be
found in Downing Street more days in the week
nor more hours in the day, than he can help.

Next to the official residence of the Prime
Minister, are the official residence and offices of
the CHANCELLOR of the EXCHEQUER.   These
premises, like the house just described, though
possessing no external attractiveness, are very
commodious in the inside.   The rooms are, for
the most part, spacious and lofty.   The furniture is scanty and plain.   Most of the apartments into which the public are admitted when
on business with the Chancellor of the Exchequer, have all the appearance of being so
many libraries : and most monotonous is the

aspect of the books. They are not only for the most part uniformly bound, but they are chiefly of one size, namely, the folio size. The standard books, if books they should be called, to be found in the Chancellor of the Exchequer's official apartments, principally consist of acts of parliament, parliamentary reports, treatises on international law, and works on other heavy and uninteresting subjects. As for works of fiction, or the effusions of the muse, you might as soon expect to find lobsters on the land, as to meet with a novel or a volume of poetry within the precincts of the office of the Chancellor of the Exchequer. Sir Walter Scott's novels are supposed to have penetrated everywhere : it is a great mistake; they have never yet found their way to the Downing Street libraries. At all events, I have not met with any one that ever discovered them in that locality. Shakspeare has been called the poet of all times and of all countries. I do not question the justice of the remark. But, if any one will hazard the hypothesis that he is also the poet of all *places*, I will undertake to demolish the hypothesis in a single sentence : he is not the poet of Downing Street. Byron may be popular enough everywhere else : he is unknown in the official library of the Chancellor of the Exchequer, or in any of the other libraries in the same locality. I doubt, indeed, if the scraps of poetry which Mr. Spring Rice has himself occasionally contributed to periodicals,—for he does, now and then, try his hand in the metrical way,—I doubt whether any of the works containing his poetical effusions, have ever found their way across the threshold of his library departments. Of this I am certain, that if they have, it must be the result of some smuggling transaction! The entrance must have been effected clandestinely; and, even after accomplishing a location there, the situation assigned them must be some obscure, some almost unvisited corner of the place.

There are several apartments in the Chancellor of the Exchequer's office, which are used as places in which that gentleman holds his interviews with deputations. Some of them are large, some smaller ; and in the selection of the room

in which Mr. Spring Rice, or any other gentleman who fills the office which he now holds,
condescends to see a deputation, that functionary is guided, in most cases, by the number of
persons of whom the deputation consists. Sometimes the apartment fixed on is on the ground
floor; at other times it is on the floor above.
Deputations are sometimes very numerous. I
have been present when from twenty to twenty-
five gentlemen have been honoured with an interview with Mr. Spring Rice. When the numbers
are so great as this, it becomes requisite to fetch
an additional supply of chairs for the parties;
for it is but justice to Chancellor-of-Exche-
quership politeness, to say, that gentlemen, on
all such occasions, are asked to take a seat.
The greatest inconvenience ever suffered by deputations, on their being located in the regions
of Downing Street, is before they are admitted
into the presence of the minister with whom
they are about to have the interview. Happy
he who, on such occasions, appropriates the
first chair that comes within his reach; for there is
not only a marked famine of these useful articles

of household furniture, in all the rooms into which deputations are shown before being admitted to " the presence ;" but the under official showing them into such apartments, not only never dreams of accommodating them with an additional number of chairs when necessary; but he does not always ask them to make use of the few that are in the place. And only fancy how unpleasant and tiresome it must be to stand, perhaps a full hour, before you are summoned into the apartment in which the minister is to receive you. In such cases I have seen members of Parliament and other gentlemen, compelled from sheer exhaustion caused by standing for some time after having walked a considerable distance, to throw all considerations of etiquette to the winds, and lean against a table, sit down on a box, or rest themselves in any other way they could.

The longest period I ever remember to have seen a deputation wait before they were admitted to the presence of the Chancellor of the Exchequer, was about an hour and a quarter. This was three years ago, when Mr.

O'Connell, followed by a tail of sixteen or
eighteen Irish members, waited on Mr. Spring
Rice, on some subject connected with river navigation,—the navigation, if I mistake not, of
the Shannon, in Ireland. As nearly as I can
recollect, the hour appointed for the interview
was two o'clock. The deputation were "punc-
tual as lovers to the moment sworn." Not so
Mr. Spring Rice. I think it was precisely a
quarter past three, making, as just stated, an
hour and a quarter which the deputation had to
wait, before the Chancellor of the Exchequer
condescended to be visible. To be sure, he
apologized for " keeping the deputation waiting
so long," and assigned a reason for the delay.
But before the deputation received the anxiously
wished-for summons into Mr. Spring Rice's
presence, they one and all evinced the most decided symptoms of impatience; not unmingled
with feelings of a nature which I shall not
name. Two or three were fortunate enough to
lay hold of as many chairs, on their being
shown into the room; and the remainder of the
deputation, *standing* on their notions of eti-

quette, *stood* on their legs, reading acts of Parliament or re-perusing the reports of their
own speeches in the " Mirror of Parliament;"
glad, to say the truth, to do any thing, or
amuse themselves in any way, as a sort of excuse for retaining their perpendicuar position so
long. Surely it is not uncharitable to suppose,
that while they were thus suffering a living
martyrdom, by standing on their legs, without
even a place to rest their elbows on, they were
inwardly wishing the Chancellor of the Exchequer in any other quarter than that in which
he was. At last nature gave way, and one by
one the deputation dropt down on boxes, piles
of Parliamentary reports, or any thing else that
held out the prospect of their being able to assume a sitting posture. Mr. O'Connell was
among the first to find out a good resting-place
for himself. He took up his temporary location
in one of the windows, which was, fortunately
for him, so planned at the lower part as to be
nearly as good as a chair. Still he, as well as
all present, betrayed unequivocal symptoms of
restlessness; and now and then gave utterance to

complaints at being detained so long. I thought
it was exceedingly unkind of Mr. Spring Rice
thus to treat so many of the uniform and zealous supporters of the Administration to which
he belonged; and it was with me a question
whether the circumstance might not issue in
Mr. O'Connell's detaching himself and party
from the Melbourne ministry. All the world
knows that it was attended with no such result.

Nature, it strikes me, intended Mr. Spring
Rice for receiving deputations. He has the
enviable knack of always seeing them bid him
good morning and quit Downing Street, with
the full conviction that he has entered into their
views, and that their wishes will be acceded to.
Does he then commit himself by making any
specific promise or pledge on the subject?
Not he. He is too cautious,—much too wary
for any thing of the kind. How then does he
contrive to leave this favourable impression, or
to produce this pleasing conviction in their
minds? Just by the everlasting smile which
plays on his countenance; by the agreeableness
of his manner; and by his speaking to them in

a way as favourable as possible to their views, without giving any explicit assurance on the subject. I never yet knew a deputation part with him without thinking they had succeeded in the object of their errand. " Oh, he'll do it!" " Oh, he's quite favourable to our views!" are expressions which are sure to be uttered by one or more of the deputation, as they reach the outside of the office. The others assent to the opinion, and thus show that they share the conviction. In how many cases has the event shewn that the impression was groundless!

The most striking instance I ever remember to have witnessed of Mr. Spring Rice's surpassing adroitness in dealing with deputations, occurred about two years and a half ago. The occasion was that of a deputation of gentlemen selected from the leading parishes in Westminster, to wait on the Chancellor of the Exchequer, with the view of procuring the repeal or the reduction of an obnoxious tax. The deputation proceeded to Downing Street with the full determination of obtaining, at all hazards, from the Right Hon. Gentleman, an explicit declaration of his intentions with regard to the particular tax in question. They were not to be put off with assurances of his taking the subject into his " careful and unbiassed consideration." They were resolved to be satisfied with nothing short of a statement of his views which should be so distinct and unequivocal as to be tantamount to an " Aye" or " No," to the question, whether he would repeal or reduce the tax, or not. They accordingly introduced first themselves, and then their subject. The oppressiveness and obnoxiousness of the tax, and the peculiar severity with which it pressed on the classes they represented, were pointed out with great clearness and peculiar emphasis, and appeals were made to Mr. Spring Rice's sense of justice, and to his " known" anxiety to avert the ruin of the parties chiefly affected. With these appeals to his better feelings, there were intermingled various complimentary observations which had a good deal of the appearance of flattery, and which were doubtless made use of with the view of cajoling or coaxing him into a declaration to the effect that the tax in ques-

tion could either be entirely abolished, or considerably reduced. But all their ingenuity went
for nothing. The bait would not "take."
They found him, as the proverb has it, "too
old a bird to be caught by chaff." He was as
lavish of his smiles as ever; the seven rings
which adorn his fingers, sparkled in all their
wonted brilliancy; he was dressed with more
than his accustomed elegance, of which fact he
seemed to be duly aware; and his words were
as smooth and honied as any that ever escaped
his lips; but though thus having all the appearance of a fine gentleman, and though no one who
witnessed his excessive politeness and extreme
plausibility, could for a moment have deemed
it possible that he could have withheld from
the deputation the satisfactory declaration they
were so anxious to obtain,—this was soon
found to be an erroneous impression. Nothing
but the usual vague expressions, which like a
King's or Queen's Speech may be understood
to mean anything or nothing, could be elicited
from him. The deputation were dissatisfied,
and entreated him to be more explicit. Without

appearing to comprehend the nature of their request, and with the same profusion of smiles and sugar-candied expressions as those with which he had sought to amuse them before,—Mr. Spring Rice, now perceiving that he was beginning to be rather closely pressed, said there were various taxes which he was desirous either to repeal or reduce; and that among such taxes there were some that would give great relief to the manufacturers and producers of certain articles. " Just allow me, gentlemen," said Mr. Spring Rice, " to show you some most beautiful specimens of fancy glass-work of Birmingham manufacture, and which, were the taxes on glass abolished, could be produced at such a price as would have the effect of keeping foreigners out of the British market. That, gentlemen, I am sure you will admit to be a most desirable thing."

There was not a member of the deputation that did not signify his concurrence in the remark.

" Well, gentlemen, just let me show you these beautiful specimens of fancy glass-work," and so saying, he proceeded to a cupboard-looking sort of place, in the corner of the room, and took out two fancy glass plates, which certainly were incomparably the most beautiful things of the kind I have ever seen.

" Are they not beautiful, gentlemen ?" continued Mr. Spring Rice, as he handed the plates to the deputation.

" They *are*, indeed," answered every one present, as the plates were circulated round the company.

" Now, gentlemen, were it not for the duty on glass, our British manufacturers would not only be able to exclude foreigners from the market, but they would display greater ingenuity and taste in their fancy articles than foreigners are capable of doing ; for they would then, by an increased consumption of the glass, have a greater inducement to exercise their skill in the production of tasteful patterns. Don't you think so?"

" We do!" was the unanimous answer.

" These are really beautiful articles," resumed the Chancellor of the Exchequer, as the two glass plates, which I should have before observed, were most tastefully ornamented with inwrought gold, bearing in some respects a resemblance to the finest gilded china,—were returned to him. Mr. Spring Rice replaced the two beautiful specimens of fancy glass-work in the locality whence he produced them, and then, after addressing a few more words to the deputation, in continuation of the praises of the "specimens," he pulled out his watch, as if intending thereby to give them a gentle hint that they had already consumed too much of his time. They took the hint, whether intended or not, though I have no doubt it was; and bidding him good morning, walked themselves out of the office, their heads filled with the " specimens," and entirely forgetful of the " obnoxious and oppressive tax," which had brought them to Downing Street. Before they had got the length of the Privy Council room, the fact flashed across their minds, that they had not, after all, succeeded in their object of eliciting from the Right Honourable Gentleman any explicit declaration as to his intentions with regard to the retention or repeal of the " odious impost." But the thought occurred too late; they could not venture to return to Mr. Spring

Rice, and though they had done so, he would
have taken care not to vouchsafe to them a
second interview. His object had been gained,
and while they were bitterly reproaching themselves with their folly, in suffering their attention
to be withdrawn by the fancy glass plates, from
the purpose of their visit to Downing Street,
he was doubtless laughing in his sleeve at the
success of his "ingenious device" for getting rid
of such troublesome customers.

When Mr. Spring Rice is in expectation of
receiving a deputation on any subject of great
importance, and has not made up his mind as
regards his future policy in reference to it, but
on which subject he is desirous of procuring
further information from the deputation,—he
makes a point of inviting Lord John Russell to
be present. I remember seeing Lord John on
several such occasions in the office of the
Chancellor of the Exchequer; and I could
not help being struck with the contrast which
the two ministers presented to each other in
their deportment. While Mr. Spring Rice was
all bustle, affectation, and self-importance, Lord

John was as stationary and unassuming as the table at which he sat. He patronized an easy chair on the last occasion on which I saw him assisting Mr. Spring Rice in carrying on an interview with a deputation. In that chair he deposited his little person, and, throwing his right leg carelessly over his left, and intermingling the thumb and fingers of one hand with the thumb and fingers of the other,—there he sat as motionless, and looking, as he usually does, as pale as a statue; his eye, however, beaming with intelligence, and his countenance indicating that shrewdness which is one of the most prominent traits in his character. His questions to the deputation were few, but they were exceedingly pertinent. I have never seen any person wishing to get at the facts and arguments bearing on a particular question, pursue a course more adapted to accomplish his end.

Of all the Chancellors of the Exchequer whom I have known, Lord Althorp, now Earl Spencer, had the largest amount of candour and straightforwardness, and the greatest simplicity of manner. He was the most unofficial and

the least courtier-like person I ever saw,
either in Downing Street, or any where else.
In his office, when Chancellor of the Exchequer, his manners were as plain and unsophisti-
cated as if he had spent all his days in fattening
cattle — an occupation, I may remark by the
way, which was far more congenial to his taste
than to preside over the financial department
of our national affairs. To breed a Smithfield
prize ox, was, and still is, the summit of his
lordship's ambition; while to prepare the annual budget was to him the most irksome task
which ever human being was called on to perform.   Never was man more out of his element
than was Lord Althorp when fate doomed him
to a local habitation in Downing Street.   Still
his unbounded good nature, and his unruffled
and unruffleable equanimity of disposition, prevented his ever betraying any uneasiness of
feeling when acting as Chancellor of the Exchequer.   Every person who had occasion to
do business with him, was not only struck
but delighted with the unaffected ease and
agreeableness of his manners.   Deputations

that went to his office for the purpose of badger-
ing him on account of his retention of some
obnoxious tax, forgot all their discontents before
they had been two minutes in his company;
and felt themselves disarmed of all hostility to
the minister. It was, indeed, impossible to be
angry or acrimonious in Lord Althorp's presence: his singularly good-natured countenance dispersed in a moment, as if by a magical
agency, the sourness which was so visible in the
visages of certain disaffected Radicals who were
in the habit of appointing themselves deputations to him, to remonstrate against real or imaginary grievances. He always listened with
the greatest patience to their representations,
or *mis*representations, as the case might be;
and then, if decided in his own mind that their
wishes could not be acceded to, he told them
so in plain terms. If he had not made up his
mind on the matter, he would intimate his intention of taking it into consideration; and if he
did intend to adopt their views from a conviction of their expediency and practicability, he
would give the deputation some implied in-

timation to that effect, by admitting the justice of their representations, and expressing his
intention to take an early opportunity of attending to them.   Such was usually the
manner of Lord Althorp when Chancellor of
the Exchequer.   In his personal appearance,
he was the same in Downing Street as he
always was in the House of Commons.   He
not only dressed with great plainness, but
had his double-breasted sandy-coloured cassi-
mere waistcoat, always buttoned up close to his
chin,—just as if braving all the rigours of a
Kamschatka winter, instead of breathing the
genial atmosphere of a comfortable room in
Downing Street.

Sir Robert Peel, when Chancellor of the Exchequer, which office, it may be remembered
he filled in 1834-35, in conjunction with that
of the Premiership, was chiefly remarkable in
all his intercourse with those who had public
business to transact with him, for a union of
dignity of deportment with the most condescending demeanour. Persons felt at once at ease
in his presence, without experiencing the slightest

tendency to a feeling of familiarity. Unlike
Mr. Spring Rice, he carefully guarded against
the utterance of any expressions which could
inspire hopes which were not destined to be
realised. He was exceedingly cautious in what
he said; I do not believe he ever committed
himself even by implication. He was a singularly excellent business man. No one ever
more thoroughly devoted himself to the duties
of his office. He threw his whole soul into
those duties. He rose early and worked late.
I myself have seen him (as I once hinted in
another work) in his office as Chancellor of the
Exchequer, a little after ten in the morning,
though the previous evening, or rather that same
morning, he had been in the House of Commons
until two o'clock, after having spoken, in his capacity of the head of the government, for upwards
of two hours in defence of the policy of his administration. It is to Sir Robert Peel's un-
wearied attention to business when in power,
coupled with his admirable business habits, that
we are to ascribe the fact of his having so
efficiently discharged, at one and the same

time, the duties of the Premiership and those
which devolve on the Chancellor of the Exchequer.

The COLONIAL OFFICE is at the farthest end
of Downing Street, having a front view, as you
enter that locality. It has a private entrance
in the right-hand corner. The public entrance
is in the centre of the house. It has rather a
better exterior than the houses just alluded to.
It has a double door, with a semi-circular glass
top, while, in the case of the offices before mentioned the door is single, without any glass top.
It has also a post on each side of the door: the
doors of the other houses have no such ornament. It is a commodious and comfortable
place inside. To get a sight of the present
Colonial Secretary is nearly as difficult as it
would be to get access to the most retired
Eastern prince. The Premier and the Chancellor of the Exchequer may, at any time, be
seen in their own offices, if the matter be
managed with ordinary skill; but he must be a
clever personage indeed, who, without a certain
rank, or filling some important situation imme-

diately connected with the Colonial Department, procures an interview with Lord Glenelg.
Nay, it is an achievement which argues more
than the average ingenuity, to obtain an interview with Mr. Grant, the brother and Secretary
of his lordship. A more inaccessible couple
than Lord Glenelg and his Secretary have
rarely presided over any of the more important departments of the public service. Scarcely
less difficult is it to obtain an answer to any
letter you may address the former. If you
write, and respectfully solicit, because your
letter requires, an immediate answer, you may
think yourself one of the favoured correspondents of his lordship, if such answer be received
within three weeks after your epistle has reached
the Colonial Office. Very possibly you will
get no answer at all. Various hypotheses have
been advanced to account for this remissness
on the part of Lord Glenelg. I shall only
advert to two of these. It is said, and by many
with a full belief in the truth of the statement,
that his lordship indulges in sleep to a very
unusual extent, and that to this circumstance is

K 2

his remissness in this respect to be attributed.
I reject this theory at once. I admit that he
usually has a very somnolent appearance; but
so far from squandering away his time by
sleeping more than the general run of men do,
I am convinced that he actually sleeps less than
most other persons. If I am not greatly mistaken, his servants will any day bear testimony
to the fact, that he is an early riser, and is late
in going to bed. I do believe that he devotes
more hours, on an average each day to public
business, than the majority of his colleagues.
If this be so, the sleepy hypothesis is demolished
at once. Another theory is, that his lordship is
indolent, which, let it be observed, is quite
compatible with his not sleeping away his time;
for a man—Lord Melbourne for example—may
be wide awake, and yet be by no means distinguished for the amount of business he goes
through. I cannot adopt this second hypothesis, any more than the soporific one, in the
sense in which it is understood. Its advocates
mean that Lord Glenelg wiles away his time in
idleness. Here I am at issue with them. I

maintain, from information privately received,
that Lord Glenelg is no idler. I contend that,
on the contrary, he is an industrious man,
though not industrious as the Colonial Secretary.
I am assured that he reads a great deal; and
that much of his time is occupied in corresponding with old acquaintances in the county of
Inverness, on matters pertaining to his property
and interests in that county. I speak from
personal knowledge, when I say that he is so
exceedingly anxious to stand well in the estimation of Highland lairds and other persons of
influence in the north of Scotland, that if any
thing occurred which he conceived likely to
prejudice him in the opinions of such persons,
he would " write by the first night's post " to the
North, and write too with his own hand, and at
very great length, with the view of setting himself right in their estimation. Let me not be
here understood as meaning to insinuate, that if
Lord Glenelg were to receive, by the same post,
a dispatch announcing an insurrection in
Canada, and a letter from a Highland chieftain,
that his anxiety to stand well in the good

graces of his Celtic correspondent, would induce
his lordship to give his earliest attention to the
letter of the latter.   I do not believe any thing
of the kind, whatever ill-natured people may
say.   I should also remark, as illustrative
of my assertion that Lord Glenelg is not the
indolent man he is so generally supposed to
be, that he devotes much of his time to theo-
logy.   I believe that, did he choose, he would
appear to very great advantage, were he to take
the field as a writer, either on controversial or
practical divinity.   Most people are aware that
some years since he used regularly to attend the
anniversaries of the British and Foreign Bible
Society, in Exeter Hall, and that on such occasions he made speeches, which for the intimate
knowledge they displayed both of doctrinal and
experimental Christianity, might have put many
of our bishops and other dignitaries of the
church to the blush.   When the Apocrypha
controversy was at its height, Lord Glenelg,
then Mr. Charles Grant, mastered all the details
of that rather intricate controversy, and ably
vindicated the Parent Institution, or the Earl

Street Committee, as the late Dr. Thomson of
Edinburgh, Dr. Brown of Berwick, now of
Swallow Street, London, and other able assail-
ants of the directors of the British and Foreign
Bible Society, used to call its directors.

But not only does Lord Glenelg devote much
of his time to theological pursuits, in so far as
respects reading theological works, but many of
his hours are spent in the composition of small
pieces of poetry of a highly religious character.
Some time ago, a northern Baronet, an intimate
friend of his lordship, shewed me a manuscript
production of his of this nature, which struck
me as equally beautiful for its religious feeling
and the character of its poetry. But Lord
Glenelg does not always content himself with
confining his poetical efforts on religious topics
to mere manuscript productions. He has not
only written, but published a number of sacred
hymns, which possessing, in addition to their
poetic beauties, the still greater recommendation of evangelical piety, several of them have
found their way into the collections of hymns
which are used in some of our dissenting

chapels in London.   In that admirable selection
of hymns made in 1836, by Mr. Josiah Conder,
at the request of a committee of the Congrega-
tional Union of England and Wales, and which
has been adopted by a number of London
congregations, will be found two hymns by
Lord Glenelg, remarkable alike for their piety
and poetry.

If Lord Glenelg does not spend much of his
time in the official residence in Downing-street,
attached to his office, the circumstance is not
so much to be wondered at in his case as in
that of some of the other members; for Lord
Glenelg's private residence is in George Street,
Storey's Gate, which is not above a hundred
yards distant from the Colonial Office.

Next to the Colonial is the FOREIGN OFFICE,
the entrance to which is not unlike the entrance
to its neighbour of the Colonial Department.
The Foreign Office is directly opposite that of
the Chancellor of the Exchequer's, so that
Lord Palmerston and Mr. Spring Rice might,
if at any time they should feel so disposed,
speak across the street from their respective

windows, to each other. The Foreign Office is, as a whole, perhaps, better fitted up and more spacious in its apartments than any of the others. One of its rooms is peculiarly commodious and elegant. I allude to the apartment in which all the Cabinet Councils are held. If the fact should not before have occurred to the mind of the reader, it may be worth being here mentioned, that all the ministerial meetings and deliberations take place in this office. Who then shall need to be told, what important measures have been first brought into a tangible shape in that room? Who shall say what has been the influence, on the one hundred and twenty millions of persons who acknowledge their subjection to British sway, of measures which have been broached, brought forward, and agreed on in one little hour, in that apartment? Could the walls speak, what disclosures would they not make respecting the circumstances under which these momentous measures were adopted by the government? If walls had ears to hear, and a tongue to speak, what revelations would they not make of treachery to

recorded protestations, and apostacy from principles loudly professed in public ! Little do the
public think that the self-daubed patriot, who
is so clamorous and declamatory on behalf of
popular principles on the hustings, or in the
senate, seizes with avidity and gladness of heart,
the first opportunity afforded him of assassinat-
ing those principles, at the cabinet council
meetings in the Foreign Office. In this room
all the foreign ambassadors are also received;
it is in fact called in a special sense, the Audience Chamber.

I could never—I do not know what other
people can do—look at, or be in, the Foreign
Office, without thinking of the tenacity with
which Lord Palmerston has kept his hold of
that office, amidst the repeated and extensive
changes which have occurred in parties and in
places within the last ten years. It mattered not
to the Vicar of Bray, who was the sovereign;
he was that sovereign's subject; and what was
infinitely better, he was the Vicar of Bray.
Equally little does it matter to Lord Palmerston, provided he be allowed to retain the Foreign

Secretaryship, who is Premier, or what that
Premier's politics are. Mr. Albany Fonblanque,
editor of the "Examiner," has written a book,
which he has called, "England under Seven
Administrations." That is precisely the number,
if I mistake not, of Prime Ministers under whom
his lordship has had the honour, for so he himself considers it, of serving his country—and
himself. A manageable conscience in politics,
as in everything else, is a mighty desirable
thing. It saves those who have the good fortune to possess it, from many serious inconve-
niences. Dying for one's country, or principles!
What could be more foolish? The thing is unintelligible. It were far more rational, if a person
were fool-hardy enough to die for anything, to
give up the ghost for one's place. Lord Palmerston will, I am sure, concur with me in this view
of the case.

The Foreign Office always brings to my re-
membrance the celebrated dispute, some seven
or eight years ago, between Holland and Bel-
gium. Why, it may be asked, does the Foreign
Office bring this afresh into my memory? Be-

cause it was in that office that Lord Palmerston
well nigh pestered the King of Holland to
death, by protocolling his majesty at so un-
merciful a rate; upwards of a hundred prolix
protocols were drawn up in that office, and fired
from it at the head of that unfortunate monarch.
To endure the breaking off of their allegiance to
his majesty, on the part of his Belgian subjects,
was no doubt a sufficiently serious calamity to
him; but I am sure it must have dwindled into
insignificance, when compared with a visitation
of such frightful magnitude as the century of
protocols.

Lord Palmerston is tolerably attentive in the
discharge of his official duties. He is not often
absent from Downing Street, when he ought to
be there. Still, even in the most pressing
emergency of foreign affairs, no consideration
will induce him to make his appearance in the
Foreign Office until he has devoted the allotted
time to his toilet. There is not a lady in the
land that attaches greater importance to the
article of dress, than does his lordship. Hence,
the many jokes which have been and daily are

expended on his personal appearance. These jokes, I should here observe, are always taken by his lordship in the best part. If those who are in the habit of calling him Cupid knew not only how little he cares, but how heartily he laughs, when that epithet is applied to him, it would not appear with such frequency in the columns of some of the Tory journals. I remember his making, in the last session of Parliament, such humorous allusions to his being called Cupid, as convulsed the House of Commons with laughter.

Lord Palmerston, it may not be amiss to mention, has the reputation of being able to converse with fluency in a greater number of the living languages of Europe than any other Englishman known to fame. Others may have a more general critical acquaintance with such languages than his lordship, but in the article of speaking them with ease, he is said to have no rival.

I am not sure whether the fact is worthy of observation, but it is a fact, that the Foreign Office is always protected by a soldier, who

performs the functions of a sentinel a few yards
from the door.   Why the Foreign Office should
have this mark of distinction conferred on it,
while neither the office of the Premier, nor that
of the Chancellor of the Exchequer, nor of the
Colonial Secretary, has any such protection
afforded them, I am at a loss to imagine.

No person accustomed to reflection can have
been in Downing Street, without thinking of
the interest which attaches to the locality, both
in the eyes of the country, and of the civilized
world.   From all parts of the British empire,
even from our remotest possessions in the East,
and from every Court to which civilization has
worked its way, despatches of the deepest
moment are daily forwarded to Downing Street;
and the answers to these despatches are in
many cases looked forward to with an intensity
of anxiety by monarchs and ministers, of which
none but themselves can have any conception.
From each of the offices in that street, though
my remarks chiefly apply to the Foreign and
Colonial Offices, bags of letters are every evening taken by a person in the service in the post-

office department, which contain communications whose importance is beyond all calculation. Were a person suffered to break open the bags, and to examine their contents, how varied and how momentous would they be found! and how conflicting would be the feelings of the parties immediately interested! There would be seen some foreign country's views defeated and hopes blasted; the wishes of another Court acceded to; a whole colony, and that too an extensive and populous one, treated with the grossest injustice; or it may be, about to have all their grievances redressed. A single sentence in one of the dispatches may avert a threatened war, or may interrupt the peace of Europe. From nations or colonies, there would be the descent to individuals. Some injured man who has stated his wrongs and demanded justice, is virtually told, if not in so many words, that he shall have no justice done him; another, perhaps, is assured that an immediate inquiry shall be instituted into his case, and redress afforded, if it be found that he has been wronged. One letter will fill the breast of some dependent individual with inexpressible joy : it appoints him to a lucrative situation.   Another epistle will almost break the heart of some other party, as it puts an extinguisher on all his fond hopes, by telling him that the official can do nothing on his behalf, which in most cases, means that he *will* do nothing for him.

So much for the various offices in Downing Street.   The Home Office and most of the other offices of importance are in Whitehall, which, I may mention for the information of those unacquainted with the localities of that particular part of London, is situated on the right hand in the broad street which leads from Charing Cross to Parliament Street.

I cannot undertake to say with confidence what the number of letters is which is daily received in all or either of the four leading offices in Downing Street.   The number necessarily varies with the state of public feeling and public opinion on particular subjects.   At times of excitement in the country, a great addition is made to the number of the Premier's corres-

pondents. When the financial affairs of the
nation wear an unpromising aspect, the Chancellor of the Exchequer finds a vast addition to
the number of communications made to him
in more prosperous times. The Secretary for
the Colonies finds matters in pretty much the
same position, in so far as he is concerned.
Lord Glenelg, I will answer for it, found what
Mr. O'Connell would call "a mighty" difference between the number of communications
he received before and after the breaking out of
the insurrection in Canada. In the Foreign
Office, the same remark holds equally good.
As a matter of course, the communications received by the Premier are much more numerous, than those received by any of the other
officials in Downing Street. I am not aware
what the average number may be which are
addressed to Lord Melbourne; but if I remember rightly, the Duke of Wellington, when
he filled the offices which Lord Melbourne now
holds, often received from 150 to 200 per day.

How can any Minister, it will be asked by
the uninitiated, continue to wade through such

a mass of correspondence. Bless the simple
souls of those who can put such a question! No
Minister ever does, or dreams of doing, such a
thing. They have severally their secretaries
whose duty it is to open and peruse all letters
addressed to them, when there is not the name
of the writer on the back to indicate that such
letters are from particular persons. The secretaries, when they have read the epistles addressed to their masters, apprize the latter of
their contents, without even producing them,
and having received a verbal answer, they
communicate such answer to the parties, the
answers always being written as if from the
Ministers themselves, and the name of the
writer for the Minister, being duly attached
to the letter. Hear this, all ye who imagine you
have only to address a letter to some person
filling some ministerial office, to have your
letter duly brought before him, and carefully
read and considered by him.

The applications which are daily made to the
leading members of the government, are often
of a most ridiculous kind. They are constantly

bored to give government situations to persons
of whom they know nothing, and of whom they
never before heard. It were well if such applications were confined to letters, because an
epistle gives but little trouble, and is easily
disposed of by giving it a location in the grate,
previous to its evaporation in flame and smoke.
But the evil of it is, that Ministers are daily
subject to annoyances in the shape of personal
applications for personal interviews relative to
individual objects. Of course, many persons
crave an interview, who never obtain it; but
there are others, who are not to be defeated in
their purpose, by a first or even second denial
to see them, on the part of the Minister with
whom they are desirous of having an interview.
One curious case of this kind, which occurred
a short time ago, comes within my own personal knowledge. The party to whom I refer,
fancying that he had made a most momentous
discovery, namely, the way in which 2,000,000*l*.
might be annually added to the revenue without the imposition of any new tax,—was naturally desirous of an interview with the Chan-

cellor of the Exchequer on the subject. Time
after time did he apply to Mr. Spring Rice for
an audience; but in every instance without
effect. The right honourable gentleman could
not, because he would not, see him.

Still he was not to be baffled in his views.
He sought an interview with Lord Melbourne,
on the ground that he had made a discovery of
great financial importance to the government
and the country, which he was anxious to communicate to his lordship. As the matter related
to the subject of finance, Lord Melbourne, as a
matter of course, referred the party to the Chancellor of the Exchequer. "But," said the other,
"he will not grant me an interview. Will your
lordship," he added, "be kind enough to give
me a note of introduction to him." Lord Melbourne, with that good nature and disposition
to oblige, which are so characteristic of him,
especially, as in this case, when he wishes not to
be troubled himself, at once acceded to the request of the party, and requested Mr. Spring
Rice to "hear" what he had got to say. Of
course, the Chancellor of the Exchequer at once

complied with the Premier's wishes. So far the object of the party was gained. But then came the most amusing part of the matter. "Well, Sir," said Mr. Spring Rice, "I understand you have made some important discovery in finance, which you are anxious to communicate."

"I have made an important discovery," observed the other, with a very consequential air; for he was always on such excellent terms with himself, as to feel thoroughly persuaded that he was more gifted, in an intellectual sense, than any body else.

"Perhaps you would be kind enough to inform me what it is?" suggested the Chancellor of the Exchequer.

"It will, sir, make an annual addition to the revenue, of two millions, without imposing any fresh tax," answered the other, adjusting his collar, with great self-complacency.

"That is an important discovery, indeed," remarked Mr. Spring Rice.

"It *is* an important discovery, sir,"

"Pray, what may be its nature?" resumed Mr. Spring Rice.

" Ah, Mr. Rice," answered the other, making a wry face, " you don't surely think I am such a simpleton as to inform you of that ?"

The Chancellor of the Exchequer gazed, for a a few seconds, in silent astonishment, on his visitor. " For what purpose, then," he inquired, " did you solicit this interview ?"

" What I mean, sir," observed the other, " is, that I will not inform you of the discovery unless you gurantee to me beforehand, that you will settle on me a pension, of at least, £1,000 a-year, in return for so important a disclosure."

Mr. Spring Rice's astonishment deepened at the cool effrontery of his visitor.

" On no other terms will I reveal the important secret," continued the latter.

" But how, sir," asked the Chancellor of the Exchequer, " could you, for a moment, expect that I should come under any such obligation as you propose, before I had learned the nature of your discovery ? Perhaps, instead of adding two millions a-year to the revenue of the country, it might not add one farthing."

" I pledge myself," observed the other, " that

it *will* be worth two millions a-year to the government of the country."

" But *I* must be satisfied on that point," remarked Mr. Spring Rice, "before I make any promise of reward. Mention your discovery, and then I shall decide whether it is worth anything or not. If it be as important as you say, you shall be most liberally recompensed by the government for making it known."

" But, sir, if I were simple enough to mention the discovery, you might pretend you had previously made it yourself, and then, after appropriating my ideas, refuse me any recompense. I must have a guarantee for the compensation I have mentioned, before I communicate the discovery."

" Sir," said the Chancellor of the Exchequer, in a very indignant tone, caused by the imputation on his personal honour, " I shall hold no further conversation with you on this, or any other subject."

Mr. Spring Rice hastily rose from his seat, and the other, seeing the abrupt and awkward conclusion to which the interview had been

brought, took up his hat and walked himself
out of the apartment.

What the discovery was which this individual
had made, or imagined he had made, still, I
presume, remains a secret in his own breast.   I
am indebted to himself for the previous facts;
but he evinced as great an indisposition to inform
me of the discovery itself, as he did in the case
of the Chancellor of the Exchequer.   He stated
that it was connected with the newspaper-press,
but beyond that fact he preserved an unbroken
silence.

But one of the most amusing anecdotes respecting interviews of private individuals with
Ministers, which consists with my own knowledge, is the following :—Some time after the
passing of the Reform Bill, and when Mr.
Hume was in the zenith of his reputation and
influence, as the friend of Liberal principles, a
licentiate of the Scotch Church, well known in
Edinburgh—though I forbear to mention his
name—taking advantage of being accidentally
two or three times in the company of the then
Member for Middlesex,—called one day at

Bryanston Square, and, sending up his card, solicited a short interview with Mr. Hume. The Honourable Member (now for Kilkenny), with his usual readiness to see an old friend, at once desired the servant to show the party upstairs. Mr. Hume's bidding was promptly done, and in less than a minute the Presbyterian licentiate, who, I should observe, without being positively insane, was what is called in Scotland, "a little crack," stood before Mr. Hume as large as life. The usual courtesies having been exchanged, which they were in a mongrel sort of language—half Scotch, half English,—the Presbyterian divine stated that his chief object in calling at that particular time on the Member for Middlesex, was to apprise him that a certain bishopric was vacant, owing to the death of the dignitary who had filled it.

"I am perfectly aware of that," observed Mr. Hume, rather surprised at the party in stating such a fact to him.

"Oh! you are aware of it then, are you, Mr. Hume?" remarked the other.

"I should suppose every body who reads the papers is so, as well as myself, for it has been stated in all the public journals."

"Verra guid," said the Scotch divine, in a strong Auld Reekie accent: "I'm glad ye are aware of the vacancy, for I have ta'en the liberty of calling on you to see if you would get me an appointment to the vacant See."

"*I* get you appointed to a bishopric!" exclaimed Mr. Hume, surprised beyond measure, and no wonder, at the extraordinary nature of the application. "What could have put that into your head?" continued the Member for Middlesex. "*I* have not the power of making bishops."

"I never imagined you had," replied the other with a coolness and collectedness of manner which were rather at variance with the hypothesis that he had what in vulgar phraseology is called "a bee in his bonnet: "I never imagined you had; but I thought that you might possibly have the necessary influence with those who have the power."

An idea occurred to Mr. Hume. Though

there is not a man in the world more innocent
of a disposition to have a joke at other people's
expense, the temptation to have a little fun on
this occasion was too powerful to be resisted.
" You are a Presbyterian," said he, addressing
himself to the candidate for the vacant See;
" and how could your conscience allow you to
embrace Episcopacy?"

" Conscience, Mr. Hume! Conscience, where
some thousands a-year are concerned!"

"Well, then, you had better apply to Lord
Grey.   He is Prime Minister, and the appointment is vested in him.

" But where is he to be seen?"

" Why, at his official residence in Downing
Street."

" Could I see him just now?" inquired the
Presbyterian aspirant of a mitre and its emolu-
ments, with considerable eagerness.

" No doubt of it," answered the honourable Member for Middlesex.

" Then I'll bid you good morning, Mr.
Hume."

L 2

" Good morning," echoed the honourable
gentleman.

The " stickit minister "—as licentiates of the
Church of Scotland, who are not fortunate to
get a church, are often called—having, as he
spoke, snatched up his hat and made his best
bow to Mr. Hume,—quitted the residence of the
latter, and proceeded with all the expedition of
a practised pedestrian to Downing Street. He
soon found out the office of the Premier, and
at once requested the porter at the door to be
admitted into his presence.

" Your name, sir ?" demanded the porter.

The name was at once given, and was forth-
with verbally communicated to Earl Grey, the
Scotch divine not being sufficiently fashionable
to sport a card. The Premier had never heard
of such a person before, and could not see him.
A message to that effect was delivered to the
applicant for the vacant bishopric; but he was
not to be so easily diverted from his purpose:
he was not thus to be defeated in his objects.
" Tell Earl Grey," said he to the bearer of the
message—and in this consisted the ingenuity of

the Scotch Presbyterian, and also the infliction of righteous retribution on Mr. Hume for the joke which he had played off at his countryman's expense ;—" tell Earl Grey that I am a particular friend of Mr. Hume's, and that I have most important communication from that gentleman, to make to his Lordship."

The message was conveyed to Earl Grey, and the Member for Middlesex being at that time one of the most zealous and efficient supporters in the country, of his Lordship's Administration, the party was at once admitted to an interview, and received with great politeness.

" I have called," said the Scotchman, after a moment's pause, and without a word in the shape of preface ; " I have called to solicit the honour of an appointment by your Lordship to the vacant bishopric of ——."

Lord Grey was so completely confounded, as to be unable for some time to utter a word. At length he said, " May I ask, sir, who you are?"

" Oh, certainly," answered the other. " I

am from Edinburgh; and am a licentiate of the Church of Scotland; but am quite willing to join the Church of England, if I can get a good living in it."

This was to Lord Grey confusion worse confounded. "I understood," observed his Lordship, after a momentary pause, "that you had some important communication to make to me from Mr. Hume!"

"Certainly, my Lord, and so I have, on a matter most important to *me*. It was at Mr. Hume's request that I came here, he having desired me to call on your Lordship, and solicit from you the presentation to the vacant bishopric."

The thought now flashed for the first time across his Lordship's mind, that the man must be labouring under a greater or less measure of mental aberration. He, therefore, with the view of getting the more easily rid of him, said he would see Mr. Hume on the subject. The other thanked his Lordship and quitted the office, thinking with himself that he was now sure of the bishopric, inasmuch as there could be no doubt that his friend the Member for Middlesex, would successfully exert his influence on his behalf, if once he and the Premier were brought together on the subject.

Only imagine Mr. Hume's surprise and mortification, when his Scotch Presbyterian friend returned to Bryanston Square, and informed him that he had used his name to Earl Grey, and that his lordship was to have a meeting with him relative to his appointment to the vacant See. Mr. Hume vowed that from that moment he should never adventure a joke, nor attempt a hoax, at the expense of any individual on earth. This was the first experiment in the jocular way he had made, and as it turned out so badly, the determination he came to that it should be the last, was just what might have been expected.

I could relate various other amusing instances, which consist with my own knowledge, of the way in which the Ministerial tenants of Downing Street are literally persecuted by eccentric or unreasonable persons into a compliance with their solicitations for an interview;

but the space I have already allotted to this
chapter renders it necessary I should now draw
it to a close.

I have only further to observe, that the present administration are anything but popular
among the inferior officers in Downing Street.
The latter say they cannot endure the face of a
Whig, especially a Whig minister. They
maintain that it is the reverse of English-like.
They institute at times very unpleasant com-
parisons between the existing Whig ministers,
and the ministers who used to inhabit Downing
Street in the good old days of Toryism. Nor
is it to be wondered at, that with at least one
portion of the servants of the powers that be in
Downing Street, the present Cabinet should be
very unpopular, when it is remembered that
that Cabinet has carried its notions of economy
to such an extent, as to discontinue the taking
in of certain papers which are opposed to them,
on the alleged ground of *expense to the nation;*
which papers had, according to immemorial
practice, been the perquisites of those servants.
These latter call this a very " unkind cut,"

especially when it is remembered what a world
of patronage these same Whigs have created in
order to provide for their own hungry friends. I
must confess that I take precisely the same view
of the matter. This peddling three-farthing economy is unworthy of any government: it is
a reflection on such a country as England. It
wears a most awkward and ugly aspect when it
is contrasted with the prodigality with which
the same parties lavish the public money on
those who are their " most obedient servants " in
Parliament or in any other sphere, where, to use
the language of that class of advertisements beginning with " Situations wanted," they have
proved themselves willing to make themselves
" generally useful."

CHAPTER V.

THE BRITISH MUSEUM.

The Building—Origin and History of the Museum—The Exhibition Rooms—Moral reflections suggested by witnessing their contents—Number of persons who visit the institution.

THE British Museum is perhaps the most valuable of all our public institutions. It is every day rising more and more into importance, and is at the same time making a corresponding progress in public favour. It is situated near the east end of Great Russell Street, Bloomsbury. Reserving the Reading Room and Library of the institution for a separate chapter, I shall in the present case, after a few historical remarks, make some observations, and communicate some facts which are not generally known, respecting the rooms which are appropriated to the wonders of nature and art.

The building itself is one of great magnitude. On entering the gate, a spacious quadrangle presents itself. On the south side is an Ionic colonnade. Directly before you is the main building, while the two wings on either hand, between the gate and the entrance to the principal building, are appropriated as dwelling-places for the officers of the institution. The main edifice was originally the mansion of the Duke of Montague, and was erected by Peter Puget, a native of Marseilles, who was brought over from Paris for the purpose. This was towards the close of the seventeenth century. The property which was called Montague House, was purchased in 1754 by the trustees of the British Museum from the heirs of the Duke of Montague, with the view of fitting it up for the reception and exhibition of the valuable library, manuscripts, and collection of curiosities in nature, art, and science, which had, the year before, been bequeathed to go-

vernment by Sir Hans Sloane, for the benefit of
the nation, on the payment of 20,000*l.* to his
heirs and successors. The library and museum
of Sir Hans Sloane, which were thus given to
the public on the condition of 20,000*l.* being
paid in return to his heirs, were supposed to
have been worth nearly 100,000*l.* He had
purchased the various books, manuscripts, and
curiosities at the cheapest possible rate, as occasion offered during the long period he practised as physician in Chelsea, and he stated
some time before his death that they had cost
him considerably upwards of 50,000*l.* The
price paid for Montague House was 10,000*l.*

But capacious as this mansion was, it was
soon found far too small for the additions of
valuable articles of various kinds which, year
after year, were made to the Museum. Repeated enlargements have from time to time
been consequently made, by erections, chiefly
at the back part of the building. Within the
last twelve or fourteen years nearly one-half
more space has been provided by additions to
the numerous buildings. The magnitude of

these may be inferred from the fact, that the expense has been little short of 300,000*l.*

Soon after the British Museum had been duly recognised as a national institution, Parliament, having obtained possession of the museum which had been collected by Sir Robert Cotton in the reign of Queen Elizabeth, and had been greatly increased by his son,— passed an act transferring his collection of books, curiosities, &c., to the British Museum, for the benefit of the nation. Independently of a library of printed books and manuscripts, including books of prints and drawings, the Cottonian collection consists of the following articles :—

Coins and metals . .	23,000
Antique idols, utensils, &c. .	1,125
Cameos, intaglios, seals, &c. .	1,500
Vessels and utensils of agate, jasper, &c. . . .	542
Anatomical preparations of human bodies, parts of mummies, calculi, &c. . ·	756
Quadrupeds, and their parts .	8,186

Birds, and their parts, eggs, and

nests 1,172

Fishes, and their parts . 1,555

Amphibia 521

Crustacea 1,436

Shells, echini, entrochi . . 5,845

Insects 5,394

Corals, spunges, zoophytes. . 1,421

Stones, ores, bitumens, salts, &c. . 9,942

Volumes of dried plants . . 334

Mathematical instruments . . 55

Miscellaneous artificial curiosities. 2,098

Manuscript catalogues of the whole Museum, thirty-eight volumes folio, and eight volumes quarto.

I have referred thus minutely to the Sloanian and Cottonian collections, because they form the basis of the splendid Museum which is now exhibited to the public, and which, though defective in certain departments, is regarded as a whole with admiration by men of all nations; and, as will be inferred from the statements I am about to make, it is worthy of all the admiration with which it is regarded.

Along with the Cottonian library and museum, Parliament, at the same time, had at its disposal 2000 volumes of books which had been appended to the Cottonian library by Major Arthur, of St. George's, Hanover Square, together with the reversion of 7000*l.* for the purpose of erecting a suitable place as a public library. This was also granted by the Legislature to the British Museum, and therefore became part of the new Cottonian foundation. Some time after this, Parliament purchased for the British Museum the entire collection of Harleian manuscripts. The collection was, at the time, the property of the Countess of Oxford, and the sum paid was 10,000*l.* In this collection there were no fewer than 40,000 original rolls, charters, and other instruments, many of which are of great antiquity, while nearly the whole relate to the political, parliamentary, and ecclesiastical history of Great Britain.

To meet the various sums thus expended in providing a National Museum, and to secure a permanent fund for its support, Parliament resolved to raise 100,000*l.* by way of lottery.

This having been done, a balance of 28,663*l.* remained after liquidating the debts incurred by purchases and repairs of the building. This sum was laid out in the purchase of 30,000*l.* three per cent. Reduced Annuities, in order to constitute a permanent fund for the maintenance of the institution. This was three or four years after the purchase of Montague House. In 1759, the repairs of the building having been completed, and the various articles being properly arranged, the Museum was for the first time opened to the public for the purposes of study and inspection.

Since this time, a great many presents of books have been made to the Museum, and several small libraries have been purchased for and added to it, to which it is unnecessary to refer in detail. Various sums of money and private collections of curiosities have also been bequeathed to it, while other collections have been purchased by Parliament. Among the gifts may be mentioned that of Sir Joseph Banks to the trustees of the British Museum. It consisted of a great number of very valuable

natural and artificial curiosities, collected in the
then newly-discovered South Sea Islands. Some
idea of the number and variety of the articles*
contained in the British Museum, will be found
in an after part of this chapter. What the entire
sum is, which must, from first to last, have
been paid for the contents of this institution, is
a point which I cannot determine; and it is one
which I suppose no one else could, as I believe
regular accounts of the money expended in the
purchase of articles have not always been kept.
If I may hazard a conjecture on the subject, I
should say the entire sum must be considerably
above half a million.

On entering the British Museum, the mind is
completely overpowered by the variety and
multiplicity of the objects which present themselves to the eye. There is, if I may so speak,
a competition among them as to which has a
preferable claim to the visiter's attention. The
result is, that many persons are so confounded

* I here exclude the books, manuscripts, &c., in the library
of this institution, as I mean to devote a subsequent chapter
to them.

with what they see around them, that they
come away without any very definite notions of
the place and its multifarious contents. Every
one has heard of individuals having a great
variety of objects set before them, and, on
being asked to make a selection for themselves,
have felt unable to decide, from the very
number and nearly equal value of those objects.
It is the same in the British Museum. The
productions of nature and art which are here
exhibited, are so varied, and are all so wonderful of their respective kinds, that one literally
feels it next to impossible to give his undivided
attention for any time to any particular object.
I need not add, that on one short visit it very
rarely happens that any one object is fully examined, or that the visiter receives that pleasure
from inspecting it, which, under other circumstances, he could not fail to have derived from
it. Indeed it is quite common to see visiters
passing on from one room to another as rapidly
as if there were nothing but the bare walls before them. To see the British Museum to
advantage, it is necessary that repeated visits

be paid to it. When one visits it two or three times, the distracting gloss of novelty in some measure wears off; the party feels his attention less distracted by the number and variety of the objects around him, and is enabled to examine every thing which presents itself to his eye with some measure of attention.

On entering the ground-floor of the Museum, the objects which present themselves to the visiter's eye are not numerous; but some of them are very interesting. Perhaps the most curious and generally attractive of these is one of the originals of Magna Charta, which is exhibited in the first room. It belongs to the Cottonian library, and is protected from the action of the atmosphere or the touch of visiters, by being placed in a glazed frame. Parts of it are considerably defaced, but other parts are as legible as if it had been the production of yesterday. The ground-floor consists of sixteen rooms; but as these are appropriated to the books, strangers are not admitted into them.

Proceeding up stairs, you are struck, on reaching the first landing-place, with a Lama

from South America.   On the second landing
place are a Musk-ox from Melville Island, and
a Polar bear; both of which are objects of
interest.   On the upper landing-place are a male
and female Giraffe, or Cameleopard, and a Hip-
popotamus or River-horse.   In any situation
these animals would have a striking appearance; in the situation in which they stand in
the Museum, their appearance is peculiarly
striking.

The first room on the upper floor contains a
great variety of most curious objects.   Among
the most interesting of these are the Esquimaux
dresses; specimens of cloth from the Sandwich
Islands, formed of the bark of the paper mul-
berry; spears, bows, arrows, and other warlike
instruments used by the natives of various
savage countries; and a number of small
carved deities from the South Sea Islands.
Who can look on the latter objects, and think
that any portion of our fellow creatures should
fall down before them, and worship them as
gods, without blushing for the ignorance, and
superstition, and credulity of the human mind,

when it has not been brought within the agency of Christianity?

The second, third, and fourth rooms on the first floor are chiefly devoted to a collection of dried plants. When it is remembered that the number of plants of one kind or other, which are now known, is under 80,000, the number in the British Museum must be regarded as very large. What the exact number is, I have not the means of ascertaining; but it is above rather than under 45,000. These plants chiefly consist of the collection made by Sir Joseph Banks. Sir Joseph's collection amounted to no fewer than 30,000. Since then a large and valuable donation of Indian plants has been made by the directors of the East India Company; not to mention additions which are being daily made by the donations of, and purchases from, private individuals. The collection of plants in our national Museum is by far the most extensive and most valuable in the world, with the single exception of that in the Jardin du Roi at Paris.

The fifth, the sixth, and the seventh rooms

are principally occupied with Sir Joseph Banks's library.

The eighth apartment is exceedingly miscellaneous in its contents. Impressions of ancient seals, vases, and vessels of every kind; busts of men, animals, and inanimate things; statues, armoury, &c., are among the productions of art which are here exhibited.

Next comes the saloon, in which the collection of quadrupeds or mammalia, to adopt the technical term made use of in the nomenclature of naturalists, is placed. In this department of zoology, the British Museum is, I am sorry to say, very deficient. The number of species perfectly well known to naturalists, and fully and accurately described, is 1200; while in our great national institution the number is only 400. This deficiency is the more to be regretted, and the less to be excused, as a collection of quadrupeds worthy of this country might be formed with great ease, and in a very short time. Nor would the expense be very serious; for though the stuffing and putting up particular

quadrupeds might be as high as 50*l*.* or even
60*l*., yet this would occur in extremely few
cases, while, on an average, the expense would
not be above fifteen or twenty shillings; and
what would 1200*l*. or 1500*l*. be, in such a case,
to a country like Great Britain?

In the ninth room the upper cases containing
various quadrupeds, are intended as supple-
mentary to the mammalia exhibited in the
saloon. The other cases of this apartment are
occupied by various specimens of crustacea,
amphibia, invertebrated animals in spirits, insects, corals, reptiles, &c. To the curious this
apartment presents a great variety of exceedingly interesting objects.

The collection of insects is very imperfect. It
is altogether unworthy of a national Museum.
Though thenumber of species which are known,
classified, and described by entomologists be
upwards of 150,000, there are only 25,000 in

* The most expensive case of stuffing and putting up an
animal of which I have ever heard, is that mentioned by Mr.
Vigors, the member of Parliament. That gentleman states
that the expense of stuffing and putting up the Giraffe in the
Regent's Park Zoological Gardens was no less than 150*l*.

the British Museum; and they are very badly
arranged. The Paris Museum contains specimens of upwards of 100,000 species, and the
Berlin Museum boasts of about 90,000.

No man whose mind is rightly constituted
can look on the specimens of the insect creation
which are exhibited in the British Museum,
though not so numerous as in those institutions
I have mentioned, without feeling his thoughts
ascend towards the Creator. Many of them
are exceedingly small, and unenlightened man
would be apt to regard them as too insignifi-
cant to be worthy of a moment's thought.
With far other feelings will they be regarded
by him who has learned to take a more com-
prehensive view of the relation which subsists
between the Source of all existence and his
works. He will find that the most diminutive
insect in this vast collection derived its being
as much from the universal Maker, and on
Him, when alive, was as much dependent for
its continued existence, as man himself. It is
true that man is destined by the Supreme Being
to fulfil purposes in the divine economy peculiar

to himself, and is consequently, in that respect, immeasurably superior to the lower creation. Still there is not an insect, nor a creature of any kind, whose being or preservation was the result of chance. Every creature under heaven was made for some special, though to us unknown, purpose. And the philosophic observer will discover, in the structure of the smallest and meanest insect, the clearest proofs of the infinite wisdom by which it was created. I have heard of atheists being converted by a careful and enlightened examination of the fearful and wonderful manner in which insects are formed. Intelligence, design, and wisdom were so manifestly displayed in their formation, that there was no resisting the conviction that it must be the work of a Divine Being.

The tenth room contains the general collection of reptiles in spirits. Of these the specimens are at once numerous and curious. To the mere naked eye many of them appear most odious; but he who can look upwards to the Source whence they all derived their being, can regard them with feelings of a very different description.

In the eleventh room is contained the general collection of fishes and corals. The species of fish of which specimens are to be seen in the British Museum is 1300. This is a goodly number.. It is greater than the number contained in any other museum in the world, with the single exception of that of Paris, which is singularly rich in its specimens of the finny tribe : for it contains no fewer than 4700 species. Who can reflect on this vast number—even supposing there were no more—of inhabitants of the watery element, without thinking of the little that mankind generally know of the variety of creatures by which the world of waters is peopled?

In the twelfth and thirteenth apartments is contained the collection of British birds and British shells, together with a small collection of birds' eggs. The ornithological department of the British Museum is, as a whole, worthy of the nation. Ornithologists have not been able, hitherto, to discover more than 4500 species of the feathered tribe, though, of course, our knowledge on this subject is as yet but exceedingly limited, owing to vast tracts of Africa and Asia, especially China, being still unexplored by European ornithologists. Of the 4500 species of birds which are described and classified, the. British Museum contains 2500 species, and the number is increasing every day. In regard to British birds, the collection in the Museum immeasurably surpasses that of any other institution in the world. Some men evince a very unbecoming disposition to depreciate every thing English, and to magnify the merits of every thing foreign. A namesake of my own, Dr. Grant, of the London University, represented, before a select committee of the House of Commons, in 1835, the whole natural history department of our national Museum as being in a most deplorable state, though the fact is manifestly the reverse; and Mr. Vigors, the member of Parliament for Carlow, stated before the same committee, that so deficient was the ornithological department of the Museum, that the collection of birds might easily be increased by two-thirds in the short space of

six months. The honourable gentleman forgets
that, according to our present knowledge of
ornithology, this would be an arithmetical impossibility; for, as already mentioned, the
number of species known of the feathered
creation is only 4500; while, at the time he
made his extraordinary statement, the number
of species contained in the British Museum
was 2300!

In the department of shells there is a very
great deficiency. The assortment is so limited,
and possesses so little value, that one could
almost wish it were not exhibited to the public.
Many private individuals, curious in such
matters, have collections four or five times
more extensive and valuable. Mr. Bowerbank's
amounts to 1200, and that of Mr. Wood, of
Suffolk, to upwards of 1000.

Next comes the long gallery, one of the most
magnificent rooms ever perhaps witnessed; its
length is three hundred and sixty feet, and it is
appropriated to the collections of minerals and
secondary fossils. The objects in this apartment are at once numerous and varied, and are

displayed to the best advantage. The collection is the most valuable and extensive in the world, and is daily increasing. The greater portion of the minerals was collected by the Right Honourable Charles Greville, and were bought, in 1810, from his family, for the sum of 13,797*l.* ; that being the value at which they were estimated by a committee of the House of Commons, guided by the opinions and advice of several of the most distinguished mineralogists in Europe.

Returning to the grand entrance, you turn to the left, and proceed through a narrow and dark passage, or rather through several small apartments, filled with old books,—to the gallery of antiquities. Five rooms (the first four and the sixth) are occupied by Greek and Roman sculptures, which almost exclusively consist of those collected by the late Mr. Charles Townly, or which formed part of the museum of Sir Hans Sloane. Mr. Townly's most valuable collections were added to the Museum in 1805, having been that year purchased by Parliament for 20,000*l.* The collection was still further

enriched, in 1814, by a number of valuable antiquities, partly of the same class, which were
ascertained to be in the Townly family, and for
which the Legislature paid 8,200*l.* The fifth room
is appropriated to Greek and Roman sculptured
antiquities, of which there is a goodly number,
of great interest and value. The seventh room
contains British antiquities. The number of
these is not great, being under twenty; but
most of them are exceedingly curious. The
eighth apartment is devoted to Egyptian antiquities. The articles in the ninth, or ante-
room, which is up stairs, are few in number, and
of a miscellaneous character, though all coming
under the category of antiquities. The tenth
room is devoted to bronzes, vases, gems, &c.,
all of which belonged to the celebrated Sir
William Hamilton, for many years the British
envoy at Naples. This collection, which is exceedingly valuable and varied, was added to the
Museum so far back as 1772, having been then
purchased from Sir William by Parliament, for
the sum of 8,400*l.*

In the eleventh room there are about sixty

antiquities, many of them singularly curious, and all coming under the general designation of Greek and Roman sculptures. The same class of antiquities is contained in the twelfth room, chiefly forming a part of the collection of Sir William Hamilton. In the grand central room, which is the next apartment as the visiter proceeds in his examination, are various antiquities; but none of them are of a nature to require a special reference to them. Adjoining this apartment is the Egyptian Saloon, appropriated, as the name implies, to the exhibition of the antiquities of Egypt. It contains nearly two hundred fragments or memorials of that country, when renowned above all the other nations of the world for its learning, its science, and its knowledge of the arts. Amidst all these exceedingly curious objects, perhaps there is not one of less antiquity than two thousand five hundred years; while most of them were the productions of men who lived three or four thousand years ago. Many of the articles contained in this magnificent collection were recovered from the ravages of time by the French, when Napoleon took possession of Egypt, and came into the possession of the English army on the capitulation of Alexandria in 1801. A considerable number belonged to the collection of the late Mr. Henry Salt, while others have been presented to the Museum at different times by various travellers.

The Phigalian Saloon next claims the visiter's attention. It is filled with a large and valuable collection of marble sculptures, the frieze of a temple whichhad been dug up at Phigaleia in Arcadia. They represent, in two sets, the combats between the Centaurs and the Lapithæ, and between the Greeks and the Amazons. They are generally supposed to have been executed under the eye of Phidias himself; and all are agreed that, if not executed under his own special superintendence, they are undoubtedly the genuine productions of his school. They were purchased, in 1815, by George the Fourth, then Prince Regent, and were by him given to the Museum. They cost that prince, in one way or other, very nearly 20,000l.

Next there is the Elgin Saloon, so named because it is the part of the Museum set apart for the famous collection of Greek sculpture made by Thomas Earl of Elgin. This is by far the most valuable and extensive collection of Grecian antiquities in the world. The number of articles is nearly four hundred. The collection was made by his lordship during the time he was ambassador at Constantinople. " It exhibits," to use the words of a writer who was well acquainted with the subject, " a great part of the exquisite sculptures that still remained in the Parthenon, or Temple of Minerva, in the Acropolis of Athens, which, if not brought away by his lordship, would indubitably have fallen into the hands of the French, or been wholly defaced by the barbarous indifference or superstitious prejudices of the Turks." For this splendid addition to the treasures of the British Museum, which was made in 1816, the sum of 35,000l. was voted by Parliament.

The Egyptian antiquities and Greek and Roman sculpture departments of the British Museum have been, and still are, of incalculable service to the interests of the fine arts in this country. The genius of the Egyptians, of the Greeks, and of the Romans of a former period, lives in these remains of their productions which have been recovered from the ruins of those places which were their most celebrated seats of art and science; and they are exhibited as models for our artists. It is gratifying to find that our young artists, and amateurs also, duly appreciate the opportunities which are thus afforded them of cultivating a taste for the fine arts. Artists come from all parts of the country to take drawings of the beautiful specimens of sculpture with which the antiquities department of the Museum abounds. Not a day passes without fifteen or twenty persons being found engaged for hours in the way I have mentioned.

No man accustomed to reflection can look on the various memorials of remote ages, with which this part of the British Museum abounds, without a deep and hallowed interest. His thoughts at once go back to the eventful periods to which those memorials point. He is struck with the advanced state in which the kindred arts of sculpture and architecture must have been in those days, compared with their state in this enlightened or " march of-intellect" age. The Egyptians, the Greeks, and the Romans were immeasurably superior to us in all that appertains to the arts in question. Not only do we see innumerable traces of the highly cultivated minds of the architects and artists of those times, in the designs which everywhere, in this part of the Museum, meet our gaze; but, even in a mechanical point of view, we are mere pigmies compared with them; for supposing we possessed the same genius, or that our taste in these matters was equally cultivated with theirs, and that we were consequently capable of conceiving those designs which they carried into execution, we have not the implements by which we could execute such designs. We know of no implements which could make the slightest impression on those extremely hard stones on which they were wont to carve, with admirable taste, such an infinite variety of figures.

Fragments of Egyptian monuments surround us while we stand in this room: the architects or scientific men of the present day know of no mechanical power by which the immense blocks of stone, of which these are parts, could have been raised in the air. This is, no doubt, mortifying to our vanity; but still the fact, we fear, must be admitted.

But the unbounded admiration with which we cannot help regarding the singularly cultivated taste of the ancients in sculpture and architecture, is not unmingled with feelings of regret that their minds should have been so deplorably debased in other respects. What could be more humiliating to the human mind, than to think that men whose attainments in the respects to which I have referred were so splendid, should yet have had such erroneous ideas on the most momentous of all matters— the matters, namely, which relate to the government of the world, and the great interests of futurity?

In this respect the Egyptians, and Greeks, and Romans, in the most brilliant eras of their history, were not a whit above the most savage or the most ignorant heathen nations of the present day. Who can survey the ruins of the magnificent temples of ancient Egypt, Greece, and Rome, or gaze on the fragments of their triumphs in the art of sculpture, which are scattered about in our national Museum, without feeling the deepest pain? Who can help blushing for poor human nature, when he recollects that the gifted individuals who could conceive and execute such designs, should be devout believers in all the absurdities of their preposterous mythology—should acknowledge from 30,000 to 40,000 gods—and should fall down and worship as deities, birds, beasts, onions, and almost every vegetable or inanimate object which crossed their path? Yet so it was. Such was, in their case, the results to which the light of nature, so much boasted of and magnified in the present day, conducted them. And so it now is, and so it ever will be, in every country and clime unblessed with the light of Revelation.

No one can look on the antiquities in the British Museum, without feeling a train of reflec-

tions arise in his mind as to the changes which
have taken place in the world since the periods
to which these antiquities point us back. I
look on a block of stone richly carved. with
Egyptian hieroglyphics, and I think of .the
moral and political vicissitudes, which not only
nations, but whole continents, have experienced
since the hand that executed those figures was
laid in the dust. I look on a fragment of exquisite sculpture, and I think of the numerous
events of unutterable importance which have
taken place since the heart of him who formed
it ceased to beat. The most momentous of all
the transactions the universe ever witnessed,
the death of the Redeemer, is one of those
events which have occurred since that time.
What vast and mighty empires have since then
crumbled into dust, leaving no trace of their
fame, glory, and power! And nations, which
were at that time sunk to the lowest depths of
degradation, being not many removes in point of
intelligence above the brute creation, are now
the most civilized and powerful on the face of
the earth. The Greek and Roman empires,

then so glorious and powerful, have for numerous ages been among the things that were;
and France and Great Britain, then scarcely
known among the countries of the earth, may
now be said to be the mistresses of the world.
And not only have new powers of great moral
and political importance since that period
started into existence, but we have now an
entire world, (America,) then unknown and
undreamed of. This, however, is a topic on
which I must not dwell.

I have thus glanced at the leading departments into which the productions of nature
and art contained in the British Museum are
sectioned. We see in many of these productions of art remarkable proofs of human ingenuity; but how shall we express ourselves in
speaking of the productions of nature, or rather
of nature's God, with which the Museum so
richly abounds! If the man of devout and intelligent mind cannot walk abroad among the
fields—cannot survey inanimate creation, without, as Burns happily expresses it, looking
"through nature up to nature's God," how

much more impossible were it to behold the
vast variety of the Deity's animated works
which are exhibited in our national Museum,
without being lost in adoration of that Intelligent Power, by which they were called into
being! What displays of divine wisdom, power,
and goodness, are there made! Let the reader
only fancy, what in the British Museum he
would find to be matter of fact, that he is surrounded with fifty or sixty thousand different
species of creatures, all fearfully and wonder-
fully made, and for every one of whose continued existence due provision was made by the
same Providence who breathed into them the
breath of life; let the reader only imagine this,
and then say, whether the thought be not calculated to overpower every intelligent and vir-
tuous mind.   The more scientific and better
informed a man is, the more will he see to admire in the structure of every creature before
him.   It is a touching and deeply affecting
though delightful thought, that not one of those
myriads of once living creatures were made in
vain, any more than are the existing species

which they respectively represent. Each individual had a certain purpose to answer in the
great economy of creation; a purpose which,
in the vast majority of cases, is hidden from us
in our present state, but which shall be fully
revealed when the light of a brighter and better
world has chased away the clouds and darkness
of the present. It is gratifying to know, that if
there are men sufficiently thoughtless and un-
devout as to look on the once animated treasures of the British Museum, without feeling
one adoring thought ascend to the throne of
the great Creator, and Preserver, and Governor
of all, there are others who pay repeated visits
to this noble institution for the special purpose
of seeing and worshipping the Supreme Being
through the medium of his works. Galen was
converted from Atheism to Christianity by view-
ing the wonderful anatomy of the human frame.
I cannot refer to individual instances of similar
conversions by means of an inspection of the
once living productions exhibited in the British
Museum; but I do think it is no great stretch
of fancy, or rather no stretch of fancy at all, to

suppose that instances of such conversions have
taken place.

It is gratifying to know that the British
Museum is yearly becoming an object of increased attention to the public. The number
of persons that visited it in 1823, when a parliamentary report was published, was 153,000.
In 1836, another parliamentary report was
published, and the number that visited it in the
previous year was, in round numbers, 250,000.
I have not learned the number that visited it
last year, but I am convinced it must have been
close on 300,000, if, indeed, it was not greater.
On the Monday of the week preceding the late
coronation, the astonishing number of 10,000
paid a visit to the Museum. On Monday there
is always a greater number of visiters than on
any other day; a fact which is to be accounted
for from the circumstance of two days intervén-
ing between the exhibitions of Friday and
Monday, while, between the other days on
which the institution is open, there is only an
interval of one day. One of the officers has
mentioned to me that the average number of

visiters per day is now about 2,500. This
would give, for three days each week, 380,000
visiters per annum. The new arrangement
made last year, extending the time for which
the Museum is to be kept open for the public,
from ten till seven during the summer months,
instead of from ten till four, has tended considerably to increase the number of visiters.
The taste for such exhibitions ought to be en-
couraged and extended, by every possible
means, by the Legislature. They have a soften-
ing and ennobling effect on the minds of all
who witness them. If the lower classes could
only be made to become partial to such sights,
every trace of their fondness for prize-fighting,
or anything brutal or barbarous, would speedily
be obliterated.

In conclusion, I have much pleasure in stating, that the administration of the affairs of the
British Museum has undergone a very great
improvement within the last two years. The
mismanagement of its affairs, of which some
years ago there were such just grounds of complaint, were principally to be ascribed to the

fact of many of the trustees never attending
any of the meetings, or in any way discharging
the duties of their office. The Parliamentary
report of 1836, which gently hinted to such
individuals that it would not be amiss if they
were to resign and make way for noblemen and
gentlemen who would make a principle of discharging the duties pertaining to the office of
trustee, has had the best effect. Some have
resigned, and others, who formerly paid little or
no attention to the affairs of the institution, are
now among the most active and efficient of its
governors. A visible improvement has therefore, I repeat, taken place within the last two
years. Every thing is now seen to the best
advantage, and new objects of interest and
value are being daily added to the collections
in the various departments. If the Museum
goes on at the same rapid rate of improvement
which it has done for the last two years, it will
in a very short time compete with any similar
institution in Europe. This ought to be with
us an object of national ambition; and it is to
be hoped that the Government and the Legisla-

ture will enter into the matter with becoming spirit. An average annual grant of 15,000*l.* or 16,000*l.* (which is all that has been given for four years past,) for the purpose of adding to the treasures in the natural history department, is altogether unworthy of a great country. The amount ought to be at least 50,000*l.* The public money could not only not be applied to a better purpose, but no application of it would meet with a more general or cordial approval.

CHAPTER VI.

THE BRITISH MUSEUM—(CONTINUED).

The Reading-Room—Admission into it—Mode of procuring
the Books applied for—Number of Readers in the Room—
Remarks on their varied Pursuits and varied circumstances
—Application to Literary Pursuits under the most discou-
raging circumstances—The Library—More liberal grants of
public money to the Library department recommended.

IT will have been inferred from the previous
chapter, that there is not a better sight in
London than the British Museum : indeed there
are few places better worth seeing in the world.
There is one department, however, of this institution of which the public hear but little, and
which those who view the other departments
never see : I allude to the Reading-room. It
is situated at the eastern part of the building,

the entrance to which is through the gateway on the right hand side as you enter. It is within a few yards of the large room appropriated to the reception of the library of George the Fourth; which that monarch gave as a present to the trustees of the institution for the benefit of the public. The reading-room of the British Museum is, I should suppose from a glance of the eye, about sixty or seventy feet in length, about thirty in breadth, and about thirty in height. At the farthest end there is a wooden partition. The space beyond this partition is usually called the inner room; it is not half so large as the other, or first room.*

No person is admitted into the reading-room of the British Museum without the written recommendation of some respectable householder, who must be known by name, if not personally, to Sir Henry Ellis, the librarian, to whom the application for admission must be

---

* The Reading-room has been removed to another part of the building since this was written. It is now at the northern part of the edifice on the east side, and is entered from Montague Place. The size and appearance, however, of the new room very much resemble the former one.

made. Sir Henry, if he approve of the recommendation, which is understood to be a virtual,
though not legal guarantee for the respectability
of the candidate, signifies the same on a slip of
paper to the under librarian, who is always in
attendance in the room, and the applicant receives a ticket or printed card, containing the
rules by which that part of the establishment is
regulated.

This card insures his admission for six
months. At the end of that time it will be
renewed, on application to the under librarian
to that effect; but very few of those who attend
the Reading-room put themselves to this trouble,
as when one is known as a reader, no questions
are ever afterwards asked him, nor obstacles
thrown in his way to the prosecution of his
literary pursuits.

When a party wishes for any book, he has to
write the title of it as given in the catalogue belonging to the room, and then append his name
to the slip of paper. The object of the party's
name being written after the title of the work
he wishes to see, is to enable one of the officers

of the establishment, who chances to bring the book, to know to whom it is to be delivered. Without this there would be great and constant confusion. The officers who are usually in the reading-room, seldom bring the books applied for, but hand the slips to others in different parts of the various library rooms ; and the latter, when they have found the book asked for, give it with the slip of paper to some other servant, who carries it himself, or gives it to some one else to carry with the slip of paper in it, to the party who applied for it. The name of the party being written on the slip, enables the officer who brings the book to find out the proper person at once.

The library, consisting as it does of nearly 250,000 volumes, besides 24,000 manuscript works, necessarily occupies many rooms. When a book, which is seldom sought for, is inquired after by any party—and such works are usually in the more distant rooms—it often requires some time to get it. In the case of very rare books, half an hour has elapsed in one or two instances, in my own case, before the work written for has been brought me. These, however, are cases which very seldom occur. Generally five or ten minutes suffice. I need not say that where there are so many volumes as I have mentioned, the reading-room can only contain a very small portion of the library. Perhaps 8,000 or 9,000 volumes may be contained in it. They are all books which are most frequently sought for. All the popular periodicals, encyclopædias, gazetteers, biographical works, histories, parliamentary documents, transactions of learned and philosophical societies, &c. are to be found in the reading-room; and as a great many of them are accessible to the readers, they can take them themselves without writing for them, or asking them through the medium of any of the officers of the establishment.

The officers of this department of the institution are all exceedingly obliging in their demeanor, and always ready to meet the views of the readers. They are also intelligent; and are often of great service in directing the parties to books, when they know the subjects which are occupying their attention at the time, which will forward their views, and with which they were themselves before unacquainted. Nothing, indeed, could be better regulated than the reading-room of the British Museum.

The number of individuals whose names are on Sir Henry Ellis's list, is nearly 6,000. I recollect hearing Sir Henry mention this about two years ago, when an acquaintance of my own was applying for admission. The immense majority of this number, however, only occasionally visit the reading-room ; some only at intervals of two, three, four, five, or six months. It can hardly be necessary to say, that were even half the number to go at once, there is not a room in Christendom that would contain them ; not certainly in a sitting or reading posture, with tables on which to lay the books they are reading, or the paper on which they are writing. I should suppose that the average number of persons who are to be seen in the reading-room of the British Museum, is under one hundred, and that from three to four hundred is the number who visit it in quest of particular books, in the course of a day. I should say that there is

N 2

not accommodation for above one hundred and thirty persons in the room, even with every economy of the space. The average number of books asked for a-day is ascertained to be about five hundred; but there are many individuals who ask for two, three, four, and sometimes a greater number of books.

In the reading-room of the British Museum, are often to be seen many of the most distinguished literary characters of the day. Campbell and Moore, and the late Mr. Godwin, with others of the most popular authors of the age, have repeatedly met together, without any previous concert, in that interesting locality. Perhaps it may be said with truth, that there are few men of distinction in modern literature who have not gone with greater or less frequency to it, to prosecute their intellectual pursuits. I have seen many individuals of eminence there on repeated occasions; and I doubt not there were others of distinction present at the time, though personally unknown to me. There are some of our modern literati who have been unremitting in their attendance in the reading-room for nearly a quarter of a century. It was stated in 1836, before a Select Committee of the House of Commons, that Mr. Hallam, the celebrated author of " The Middle Ages," had been a regular attendant for nearly that length of time.

The proportion of ladies to gentlemen, who are in the habit of frequenting the reading-room of the British Museum, is exceedingly small. I should say, that on an average there is not above one lady for forty individuals of the opposite sex. I do not remember to have ever seen more than five or six ladies present at once.

The reading-room of the British Museum has been fitly compared to a literary workshop. Perhaps the phrase, " literary manufactory," would be still more expressive. In it are to be seen persons engaged in every variety of literary occupation. There is not a field of science or literature that cannot boast of its industrious cultivator there. I have often been struck with the variety of subjects embraced under the general term literature, when seeing the books which lay on the tables before me. In fact, I

had scarcely before supposed there were so
many different branches of human knowledge.
And yet every one was cultivating his own
particular department, with as much assiduity
and enthusiasm, as if it were the only department to occupy the human intellect. It has
often occurred to me as an interesting reflection,
to think of the great number of works, on every
variety of subject, which are always going on
in the limited space of that room. Every one
is busy with his own work: his attention is
entirely absorbed by it. He never passes a
thought on other persons, or the topics with
which they are engaged. Individuals may
indeed be, and there are many who often are,
in that room, who for hours together are all but
unconscious that there are any other persons
present but themselves. And yet all this while
there are perhaps a hundred other individuals
in the place, pursuing, with greater or less
eagerness, their various objects. Works, as
already mentioned, are thus at all times " pro-
gressing," as the Americans say, in every department of human knowledge. Let any one

try how many branches of learning he can call up to his mind, and then let him fancy he sees some individual most assiduously applying himself to the production of some work or other bearing on such branch of learning, and he will be able to form some idea of the varied occupations of those who frequent the reading-room of the British Museum.

Notwithstanding the variety of literary pursuits which are followed by the frequenters of this room, and the number of persons usually present, the most perfect quietness and order prevail. So great, indeed, is the silence which usually reigns in the place, that one may prosecute any subject requiring close thought with nearly as much advantage as if he were shut up in an apartment by himself. There is scarcely any speaking, under any circumstances; and when one individual does utter a word or two to another, it is always in a whisper. The only sort of noise, worthy of the name, which ever occurs, is caused by the occasional incautious moving of a chair, or the accidental falling of a book; but before one has been in the habit of attending the place any length of time, his ear gets sufficiently accustomed to this, to become almost unconscious of it. I know many who are so wrapt up in abstract contemplation, or who are so eagerly engaged in the application of all the powers of their minds to particular subjects, that they are altogether unconscious of any such external noise.

What has often grieved me to think is, that there should be so many persons of cultivated taste, all applying the undivided energies of their minds to the production of a work on some particular subject; and yet that, after doing this for many months, in some cases for years, their labour and their talents should all go for nothing. The work, when it does appear, brings them neither reputation nor profit. It may never be heard of beyond the limited circle of their own personal acquaintances; it falls still-born from the press. Such is the ill-timed destiny of innumerable authors. He whose fate it is, must indeed have strong nerves if it do not give a severe shake to his mental constitution. I can conceive of nothing more trying

to a susceptible mind—and the minds of authors
are generally so—than that a work which had
incessantly occupied one's thoughts for years,
and in the preparation of which he had been
for years constantly employed, should not on its
appearance excite the slightest interest.   The
mortification in such a case is more severe, the
disappointment more bitter, because the author
had fondly hoped it would excite a sensation in
the world on its publication; for this is a
feeling which is, I believe, shared to a greater
or less extent by every literary man engaged in
laborious works.   Severe criticism has killed
many an author.   Henry Kirke White and
John Keats are not the only persons who have
fallen victims in modern times to a heartless
and unjust system of criticism, though their
names may be those most generally known in
this respect.   As, then, every one who knows
any thing of the feelings of an author must be
aware, that utter neglect is far more trying to
the nerves than severity of criticism, the
assumption is a justifiable one, that many
unfortunate authors, though their names are

unknown to us, have had their hearts completely broken, and have eventually dropped into their graves, in consequence of the utter frustration of all their hopes, the dispersion of all their fond imaginings, caused by their works falling still-born from the press. Instances consist with my own personal knowledge, of authors having felt so keenly the failure of works which only cost them a few months' labour in the preparation, that they have never afterwards ventured to look their literary friends in the face, but have as carefully kept out of their way as if they had committed some crime of serious magnitude against society. How great then must be the shock which the person's mind receives whose work, in the production of which years of his life have been spent, falls into oblivion the very hour in which it has been published! If such a case could be aggravated, it would be in those instances, unhappily too numerous, in which all an author's pecuniary prospects have been blasted by the fate of his book.

This train of reflection has often suggested

itself to my mind when I have thought of the
literary men I have witnessed writing away for
years without the intermission, perhaps, of a
day, in the reading-room of the British Museum,
from its opening to its close, in the preparation
of some laborious work. I have thought of the
probable fate in reserve for their labours, and of
the heart-sickness, if happily nothing worse,
consequent on that unlucky fate.

It is Sterne, I think, who gives a graphic
description of the care-worn expression of
countenance and pale complexion of the literary
student. Poets and novelists have all given
vivid portraitures of the pale and emaciated
personal appearance of the man who applies
his whole soul to intellectual pursuits. There
are living originals occasionally to be seen in
the reading-room of the British Museum, which
surpass any mere portrait of the poet or novelist.
The elder D'Israeli, in his " Calamities of
Genius," refers to a striking instance of the
kind, which came under his own notice. Though
not in the habit of quoting from other authors,
my object being, in most of my works, to give

information which is nowhere else to be had, the case narrated by D'Israeli so forcibly illustrates what I have said above, that I am induced to give it.

" My acquaintance," says that writer, " with an unfortunate lady of the name of Eliza Ryves was casual and interrupted; yet I witnessed the bitterness of hope deferred, which maketh the heart sick ! She sank by the slow wastings of grief into a grave, which probably does not record the name of its martyr of literature.

" She was descended from a family of distinction in Ireland; but, as she expressed it, ' she had been deprived of her birth-right by the chicanery of law.' In her former hours of tranquillity she had published some elegant odes, had written a tragedy, and comedies; all which remained in manuscript. In her distress, she looked to her pen as the source of subsistence; and an elegant genius, and a woman of polished manners, commenced the life of a female trader in literature.

" Conceive the repulses of a modest and delicate woman in her attempts of appreciating

the value of a manuscript with its purchaser.
She had frequently returned from the book-
sellers to her dreadful solitude to hasten to her
bed, in all the bodily pains of misery—she has
sought in uneasy slumbers a temporary forget-
fulness of griefs, which were to recur on the
morrow.

"Elegant literature is always of doubtful
acceptance with the public, and Eliza Ryves
came at last to try the most masculine exertions of her pen. She wrote for one newspaper
much political matter; but the proprietor was
too great a politician for the writer of politics,
for he only praised the labour he never paid:—
much poetry for another, in which, being one
of the correspondents of Delta Crutca, in payment of her verses she got nothing but verses.
The most astonishing exertion for a female pen
was the entire composition of the historical and
political portion of some Annual Register. So
little profitable were all these laborious and
original efforts, that every day did not bring its
'daily bread.' Yet, even in her poverty, her
native benevolence could make her generous;

for she has deprived herself of her meal, to as-
sist an unhappy one who lodged above her.

" Advised to adopt the mode of translation,
and being ignorant of the French language, she
retired to an obscure lodging at Islington, which
she never quitted till she had produced a good
version of Rousseau's ' Social Compact,' Ray-
nal's ' Letter to the National Assembly,' and
finally, translated De la Croix's ' Review of the
Constitutions of the Principal States in Europe,'
in two large volumes, with intelligent notes.
All these works, so much at variance with her
taste, left her health much broken, and a mind
which might be said to have nearly survived
the body.

" Yet, even at a moment so unfavourable,
her ardent spirit engaged in a translation of
Froissart.   At the British Museum I have seen
her conning over the magnificent and volumi-
nous manuscript of the old chronicler, and by
its side Lord Berners' version, printed in the
reign of Henry VIII.   It was evident that his
lordship was a spy on Froissart, to inform her
of what was going forward in the French

camp; and she soon perceived, for her taste
was delicate, that it required an ancient lord
and knight, with all his antiquity of phrase, to
break a lance with the still more ancient chi-
valric Frenchman. The familiar elegance of
modern style failed to preserve the picturesque
touches, and the native graces of the chronicler,
who wrote as the mailed knight combatted—
roughly or gracefully, as suited the tilt or the
field. She veiled to Lord Berners, while she
felt it was here necessary to understand old
French, and then to write in good English.
During these profitless labours hope seemed to
be whispering in her lonely study. Her comedies had been in the possession of the managers
of the theatres during several years. They had
too much merit to be rejected, perhaps too
little to be acted. Year passed over year, and
the last still repeated the treacherous promise
of its brother. The mysterious arts of procras-
tination are by no one so well systematised as
by the theatrical manager, nor its secret sorrows
so deeply felt as by the dramatist. One of her
comedies, ' The Debt of Honour,' had been

warmly approved at both theatres, where probably a copy of it may be still found. To the
honour of one of the managers, he presented
her with a hundred pounds on his acceptance
of it. Could she avoid then flattering herself
with an annual harvest?

"But even this generous gift, which involved
in it such golden promises, could not for ten
years preserve its delusion. 'I feel,' said Eliza
Ryves, 'the necessity of some powerful patronage to bring my comedies forward to the
world with *eclat*, and secure them an admiration which, should it even be deserved, is
seldom bestowed, unless some leading judge of
literary merit gives the sanction of his applause;
and then the world will chime in with his
opinion, without taking the trouble to inform
themselves whether it be founded in justice or
partiality.

"The character of Eliza Ryves was rather
tender and melancholy than brilliant and gay,
and, like her bruised fortune, breathing sweet-
ness when broken into pieces. She traced her
sorrows in a work of fancy, when her feelings

were at least as active as her imagination. It is a small volume, entitled, 'The Hermit of Snowdon,' a tale formed on a very delicate, but uncommon act of the mind of fastidious refinement. Albert, having felt, when opulent and fashionable, a passion for Lavinia, meets the kindest return; but, having imbibed an ill opinion of women, from his licentious connexions, he conceived they were slaves of passion or of avarice. He wrongs the generous nature of Lavinia by suspecting her of mercenary views; hence arise the perplexities of the hearts of both. Albert affects to be ruined, and spreads the report of an advantageous match. Lavinia feels all the delicacy of her situation; she loves —but 'never told her love.' She seeks for her existence in her literary labours, and perishes in want.

" In her character of Lavinia, the authoress, with all the melancholy sagacity of genius, foresaw and has described her own death! The dreadful solitude to which she was latterly condemned, when in the last stage of her poverty; her frugal mode of life, her acute sensibility,

her defrauded hopes, and her exalted fortitude.
She has here formed a register of all that occurred in her solitary existence.   I will give
one scene—to me it is pathetic, for it is like a
scene at which I was present.

   " Lavinia's lodgings were about two miles
from town, in an obscure situation.   I was
shown up to a mean apartment where Lavinia
was sitting at work, and in a dress which indicated the greatest economy.   I inquired what
success she had met with in her dramatic pursuits.   She waved her. head, and, with a melancholy smile replied, ' that her hopes of ever
bringing any piece on the stage were now entirely over; for she found that more interest
was necessary for the purpose than she could
command, and that she had for that reason laid
aside her comedy for ever.'   While she was talk-
ing, there came in a favourite dog of Lavinia's,
which I had used to caress.   The creature
sprang to my arms, and I received him with
my usual fondness.   Lavinia endeavoured to
conceal a tear which trickled down her cheek.
Afterwards she said, ' Now that I live entirely

alone, I show Juno more attention than I had used to do formerly. *The heart wants something to be kind to.* And it consoles us for the loss of society to see even an animal derive happiness from the endearments we bestow upon it.' "

D'Israeli adds, that this unfortunate young lady died soon after writing the above passage. I have given her case because it is an everyday one, though the world seems to be little aware of the fact. Those only whose pursuits have led them into an extensive intercourse with such as live by their literary labour, can have any conception of the disappointed expectations, the heart-sickness of hope deferred, the physical destitution, and the broken spirits, which arise from the rejection of authors' works on the part of publishers, or the neglect of the public, should their works ever see the light. Instances of this kind are numerous in the history of the reading-room of the British Museum.

I could give in detail several other instances of a similar nature; but in cases where the parties are alive, it would be improper to make even a general reference to them.

It is curious to witness the enthusiasm which some literary men display in expounding and defending some wild theory, which even were it a sound one, could be of no practical utility whatever. But the more wild and visionary an hypothesis is, it will generally be found that its votaries are the more thoroughly convinced of its truth, and the more zealous in its defence. The reading-room of the British Museum has seen many martyrs to an enthusiasm in favour of extravagant theories, which, even had they been sound, could have been of no practical advantage to philosophy, science, or society. I may mention one instance of this kind. I allude to the case of the late Henry O'Brien, author of a work on the "Round Towers of Ireland." That clever and learned, though visionary young man, was seized with a very extraordinary crotchet respecting the origin of the round towers of his native country, and, with the view of establishing his hypothesis, he applied himself with a consuming anxiety

and application of mind, to the perusal of works
on the subject in the British Museum. Before
his labours were finished, it was seen by those
who knew him that his incessant application
to literary pursuits, in conjunction with his enthusiasm in favour of his peculiar notions on
the subject just mentioned, was undermining
his physical constitution. He lived to see his
book, developing and defending his theory,
published; but he did not long survive. His
premature end was most probably accelerated
by the very harsh manner in which his work
and himself personally were treated by the
critics, coupled with the fact of its having, notwithstanding all the labour he had expended
on it, met with no sale worthy of the name.

I have known others, again, waste years of
their time in incessant application to literary
research in the British Museum, and yet never
succeed in meeting with a publisher to bring
before the world the results of all this amount
of labour; while their own means would not
admit of their publishing the book on their
own account. I doubt not that there are many

valuable works which are for ever lost to the world from these causes. Such individuals, in the majority of cases, have either fallen eventual victims to their disappointments, or they have entirely abjured literary pursuits, except, merely, perhaps, as an occasional source of recreation.

I have been surprised, on the other hand, at witnessing the fortitude with which some literary characters have borne up under repeated and severe disappointments in their endeavours to acquire for themselves a prominent place in the republic of letters. And what is worthy of mention is, that, so far as my own personal observation goes, I have seen much more of this moral fortitude, this hoping against hope, exhibited by females, than by those of our own sex.

I know one who has spent years of her existence in the production of a work, and who used to be seen constantly in the reading-room of the British Museum, living on little better than chameleon's fare, that she might indulge her passion for book-writing; and yet, though her book has been finished for two years, and she has, through the intervention of literary friends of distinction, tried every publisher in London, with the view of getting it out, without success,—she still clings to the confident hope that it will by-and-bye be brought before the world and meet with the most signal success. Dr. Johnson, or somebody else, once said, that half the blessedness of life, even as regards the present world, springs from hopes which are not destined to be ever realised. . This, I am satisfied, having seen the manuscript, is a hope which will never be realised. Still, as the delusion is a pleasing one, and is likely to be as lasting as the lady's existence, it were a piece of gratuitous cruelty to try to undeceive her. She once mentioned to me, that the most celebrated phrenologist of the present day—she is herself a phrenologist—told her on one occasion, after having examined. her cerebral development, that the organ of hope was so large that it was worth at least 500*l.* a-year to her. As she has not a fourth of that sum in what commercial men call hard cash, it is a very fortunate circumstance for her that she possesses this very

handsome annual income in the shape of a
particular craniological development.

I used often to meet with another—one of
our own sex—who was blessed with an equally-
abundant supply of the commodity of hope.
There was, however, this difference between the
two, that while the lady was a person of great
talents and a most cultivated mind, the other
could lay no admissible claim to either. Having
the advantage of some money, and not meeting
with any one who would undertake the publication of his works; which, I should state, were
all compilations, the result of very hard labour
though very badly executed,—he became his
own publisher. But, alas! the books, though
published, never sold. One after another fell
still-born from the press. Still he persevered
for years, compiling, printing, and publishing,
boldly maintaining that the reason why his
works did not sell was, that their merits were
too great to be at once appreciated. He tenaciously, however, clung to the conviction that
" full justice would be one day done him," and
everlastingly quoted the case of Milton's " Para-

dise Lost," as one precisely similar to what his own would turn out to be. " One morn," some months ago, " I missed him on the accustomed hill," and have not seen or heard of him since; whether he had squandered away all his money in paper, printing, and advertising, and found his hopes vanish as his cash disappeared, I have not the means of knowing; though I think the hypothesis an exceedingly probable one.

Little do the readers of works requiring re-search know what amount of labour is some-times required before the authors have succeeded in ascertaining or clearing up a certain point. There are instances on record in the history of the reading-room of the British Museum, in which literary men have spent a whole week in the search after some particular fact, or admis-sible authority for some fact, and yet have not found it, after all. I myself know linguists who have spent several successive days in that room, in tracing out the root whence some particular word has been derived. People talk of manual labour: it is not half so exhausting or oppressive as this. West India slavery, I am assured by

some literary men, could never, even in its worst
state, have been at all comparable with this species
of mental exertion. To the reader all appears
smooth and easy : could he only form an ade-
quate idea of the anxiety and exhausting effort
it cost the poor writer to hunt out, to use a
sporting phrase, some of the matter which the
book contains, authors would receive a greater
share of popular favour than they sometimes do.

Perhaps there is no portion of the public money
which is better appropriated than that which is
devoted to the support of the British Museum,
considered as a general institution. That part
of the sum annually voted by the House of
Commons to defray the expenses of the reading-
room and library, is applied with peculiar advantage to the public. The utility of this part of
the institution is singularly great. The extent of
it may be best estimated by trying to form some
idea in one's own mind as to what would be the
injury to British literature and British statistics
of a practical kind, which would ensue from its
destruction. The precaution taken against any
calamity of this nature by means of fire, by re-

fusing ever to let light of any kind, or under any pretext, into it, is deserving of all praise; and it is one which, it is to be hoped, will never cease to be taken. To have the place open from nine o'clock in the morning to four in the afternoon all the year round, and from nine in the morning to seven in the evening in the months of May, June, July, and August, is surely affording opportunity enough to the great body of literary men to prosecute their various inquiries; and if there be some persons whose convenience, owing to their other avocations, those hours do not suit, why then, all that can be said on the subject is, that the convenience of a few individuals must give way to the general good.

I have already stated that the British Museum was instituted in 1753. The library, like most of the other departments of the institution, had its commencement in the acquisition of an extensive collection of manuscripts and printed works which belonged to Sir Hans Sloane; to a suggestion in whose will the origin of the Museum is to be ascribed. From its

institution up to the present time, it has been
regularly increasing its stores of manuscripts
and printed books. The principal source
whence it receives its constant additions to its
collection, is that of the privilege it has of
demanding a copy of every new work published
in the United Kingdom. This privilege was
conferred on it in 1767, a few years after its
institution, by George the Second, on which
occasion that monarch presented the magnificent gift of the library of the Kings of England,
which included the libraries of Henry Prince of
Wales, Archbishop Cranmer, and other distinguished individuals.

Since that period, the library of the British
Museum has been enriched by various gifts of
splendid collections of works.   In 1763, George
the Third made it a present of a large collection
of pamphlets and public papers, published
during the eventful years which intervened between 1640 and 1660; which collection had
been commenced by Charles the First.   To the
gift of the library of George the Third, consisting of 90,000 volumes, made to the Museum in

1823, I have already referred. Besides these large presents, a great many literary men have left their valuable, though much less extensive, libraries to it. The number of books purchased by the trustees is inconsiderable, compared with the number which have been derived from the sources I have mentioned. In only a few cases have private libraries been purchased. Until within the last few years the average annual amount of money expended on books for the British Museum did not exceed 200*l.*; within five or six years it has been about 1000*l.* This parsimony in the purchase of books for such an institution as the British Museum, is unworthy of this great nation.

An impression is pretty generally entertained that the library of the British Museum is the most extensive and valuable extant. I wish, for the honour of the country, the impression were a correct one; unfortunately, however, it is not so. There are no fewer than nine* libra-

* In this number I do not include the library of the Vatican at Rome, there being so many conflicting statements as to its extent. This difference of opinion arises from the non-exist-

ries in Europe more valuable and extensive than the national library of Great Britain. The King's Library, in Paris, by far the largest in the world, contains the immense number of 700,000 volumes. Even the Library of Munich, a place of which one seldom hears, can boast of its 500,000 volumes. What may appear still more surprising, Russia, barbarous and despotic as that country always has been, has its 400,000 volumes in the national library at St. Peters-burgh. Copenhagen, too, has an equally exten-sive library. Vienna estimates the number of volumes in its library at 350,000; while Naples, Dresden, and Gottingen, severally lay claim to 300,000 volumes. Lastly, there is Berlin, with its 250,000 volumes; while the British Museum can boast of no more than 240,000 volumes.

This is not as it ought to be: it is discredit-able to Great Britain that any other country, especially countries so far behind us in civiliza-tion, literature, population, and wealth, should

ence of a catalogue. I think, however, there can be little question that the library of the Vatican is as extensive as that of the British Museum.

so far surpass us in the article of a national library. Where, it will be asked, does the blame rest? It rests in two quarters; first, with the House of Commons, and, secondly, with the trustees of the Museum. The House of Commons has always been most illiberal in its votes of money to enrich the contents of the Museum generally; while the trustees have somehow or other evinced a desire to expend the money so voted in the purchase of antiquities, curiosities, objects in natural history, &c., in preference to increasing the library. This is deeply to be regretted; for the library is undoubtedly to be regarded as by far the most important department of the institution. I have reason, however, to believe that cause for this regret will not exist much longer. If I am not mistaken, the legislature will henceforth be much more liberal in its votes of money for the general interests of the Museum, and that a fair share of the money thus voted will be expended in the purchase of valuable additions to the library. This is the only way in which we can ever hope to rival the other leading

European libraries. They are severally supported by large sums of money granted by the governments of the various countries; and consequently have been enabled, even in cases where the libraries were instituted long posterior to that of the British Museum, so far to surpass us in the extent, variety, and value of their literary collections. At present we are only adding to the library of the British Museum at the rate of from 4000 to 5000 volumes a-year, while some of the libraries to which I refer are receiving annual additions to the extent of from 20,000 to 25,000 volumes.

CHAPTER VII.

THE NEWSMEN.

Their supposed Number—The Arduousness and Nature of
their Duties—Their Uproarious Disposition—The Expedi-
tion with which they Deliver the Newspapers—The rough
Reception they often meet with from their Customers—
Their Evening Duties—Their great Usefulness, and the
Claims they have on the Public Consideration.

THERE is one class of persons in the metropolitan community, which, so far as I am aware,
exists nowhere else; certainly not in Great
Britain. They are a body of individuals of
whom every one has heard, but of whom very
few persons know any thing. My reference is
to the Newsmen. The Newsmen are a class of
persons through whom all the newspapers
published in the metropolis are put, in the first
instance, into circulation. They are a most in-

o 5

dustrious body of individuals, and contribute very largely to the enjoyments of the entire population of the empire.

The Newsmen are, as far as can be ascertained, about five hundred in number. Most of them have one or more boys in their employ; and those whose business is not sufficiently extensive to enable them to employ boys, are often obliged to call in the aid of their wives—always, of course, assuming they have wives—in the delivery of the papers. The Newsmen purchase all their papers, either direct at the offices of the different journals, or at one of the three or four wholesale houses which exist in their own trade. The Newsmen get all the papers for which they charge their customers five-pence, for four-pence ;—one penny on each paper being thus all that they have to maintain themselves, after paying the expenses consequent on their business, and running the risk of bad debts. It will be seen from this that the proprietors of London newspapers do not, like those of the provinces, get the prices marked on them, and at which they are sold to the readers, but that one penny is deducted from the amount. They are not, however, on a more unfavourable footing than the proprietors of provincial papers on this account; they give no credit, and consequently are not subject to bad debts. Between the long credits given in the provinces, and the bad debts to which the proprietors of papers are there subjected, they would not be in a worse position were they put on the same footing as the proprietors of London newspapers.

Perhaps there are few callings in London more arduous than that of the Newsmen. They usually rise at five o'clock in the morning at all seasons of the year, and in all sorts of weather. This is necessary in order that they may deliver morning papers in sufficient time to their customers. A little before six they begin to muster strong at the offices of the various morning journals. And a more uproarious or merry set of persons, notwithstanding all their hard trudging through town, is nowhere to be found. They are all alive, or, as Mr. O'Connell would say, áll " agitation," from the time they assemble in any considerable number, until they have got their papers. They not only keep constantly jostling each other about, but are excellent hands at playing all sorts of tricks with one another. Nor are they by any means niggard of their jokes. Their witticisms, such as they are, are scattered about in great profusion, and it is something, certainly, to get made up in quantity what is lacking in quality. Those of them, especially the younger portion of the class, who cannot even by accident stumble on a joke, contrive by some means or other to contribute their share to the general liveliness of the scene—most frequently by a very powerful use of their stentorian powers. By way of still greater variety, it is by no means an unusual thing to witness something in the shape of a little sparring, though happily seldom ending in any serious consequences to either party.

The time for seeing the uproarious capabilities of the Newsmen to the greatest advantage, is when there is a late publication of any of the most extensively circulated journals. Then

their noise, their exclamations, and the rapidity
of their movements backwards and forwards
reach what some people would call the acmé of
perfection. The little rascals of boys, especially, are all tongue and motion together.
Neither their lungs nor their bodies are suffered
to enjoy a moment's repose ; in fact, it looks as
if the little fellows could not survive a second,
were they to remain quiet that length of time.
Occasionally, they evince a strong disposition
to quarrel with, and abuse, each other; but the
main current of their indignation is generally
directed against all and sundry connected with
the lazy journal. Editors, compositors, printer,
and publishers, all receive their respective
modicums of what these juvenile personages
call " thundering abuse." The scene exhibited
outside the office, or inside, if they can gain
admission on such occasions, is one which altogether defies description. If there be a person
whose " vocal taste" is so much out of the
beaten track as to love a confusion of sounds,
the door of a morning newspaper-office at such
a time, is the place where it may be gratified.

It is well if some of the more impatient and
least manageable portion of the assemblage do
not break out into acts of violence. A good
many years ago, the Newsmen did become so
restive in consequence of the late publication of
a journal, and did afford such unequivocal indications of the extremities to which they were
prepared to resort, that the printers, in order to
pacify them, were obliged to put into the paper
nearly a column of what is technically called
" pie ;" which means that the types are all in
such a mass of confusion that they not only do
not make rational sentences, but in very few
instances even words.   The public not being
accustomed to such specimens of typography,
were perfectly puzzled to know what could be
the cause of the circumstance, until, on the
following morning, an explanation was given in
the editorial department.   On a very recent
occasion the Newsmen gave another proof of
their disposition not to submit passively to
very late publications of the journals, by breaking the windows of one of the offices in which
an offence of the kind was committed.

It is but justice to them, however, as a body,
to say, that only a portion of them have been
parties to these little out-breaks. Taken in the
aggregate, they deserve all praise for the
patience and passiveness with which they await
the publication of a paper when much beyond
the usual time; for little do the public know the
inconvenience to which, in such cases, they are
put. In the first place, when they see that the
publication of a particular journal is to be late,
they must go and deliver all the papers which
are published at the usual time; otherwise they
are sure to incur the displeasure, and very probably lose the custom, of those who take in
such papers. This, of course, imposes on them
the necessity of going over the same ground a
second time when the paper which was late has
appeared; and, as might be expected, compels
them to make almost preternatural exertions in
order that they may get the morning-paper part
of their business through in time for entering
on that part of their labours which commences
with the publication of the evening papers.
But even this, bad enough as it in all conscience

is, is not the only evil consequent on a late
publication of a morning journal. The readers
of that particular journal abuse them without
measure or mercy, upbraiding them as careless
and lazy dogs, and holding over their heads the
threat of the loss of their patronage on a repeti-
tion of the offence; all the while assuming that
they, poor fellows, are the transgressing parties.
The Newsmen try to explain, and to put, as they
say, the saddle on the right horse; but they
always find it of no use; they only aggravate
the evil; for you may just as soon expect to
reason effectually with a man who is the victim
of what Lord Bacon calls " the rebellion of the
belly;" which means a man who is suffering the
agonies of hunger,—as with the person who has
been denied his morning journal at the usual
hour.   Newspapers are now become one of the
necessaries of London life.

The moment the Newsmen receive their
papers, they run away with them, in large bun-
dles, under their arms, or over their shoulders,
as the case may be, in all directions, " drop-
ping" them, to use their own phraseology, as

they go. The rapidity with which the Newsmen travel, or rather run, over London in the mornings, is incredible. Within little more than an hour after the impression of a particular journal has come from the printing machine, the paper is in the hands of readers at the remotest extremities of the metropolis. The arrangements of the Newsmen in this respect are admirable, and the manner in which those arrangements are carried into effect, is equally worthy of praise. The Newsmen are the real business-men after all. And then they are all feet and hands to carry out their plans. There are no lazy, creeping personages among them. No man need commence the business of a Newsman who has not got a couple of first-rate legs, and who does not at the same time possess the requisite spirit and enterprise to put the capability of those legs duly to the test.

The Newsmen, for the most part, when the publication takes place at the usual time, complete their delivery of the morning papers about eight o'clock. But their labours do not then cease: in one sense, indeed, they may be said

to be only commencing. As soon as they have
taken a hurried snatch of breakfast, they begin
to deliver papers to parties who are not subscribers, but who merely pay a penny for an
hour of a particular journal, that journal being
then returned to the Newsman. The poor
Newsman, either himself or by some of his
boys, delivers this paper at a house, it may be
some considerable distance from where he himself resides, and then calls for it again after the
hour has expired ; and all, as the showmen say,
" for the small charge of one penny." The
paper thus got from one reader is given for the
same " small charge " and for the same period
of time, to another; the industrious Newsman
delivering it and again calling for it when the
hour has expired. The same process is repeated
perhaps from eight o'clock in the morning to
three or four in the afternoon,—thus keeping
the Newsman constantly on foot. But to form
any idea of the amount of labour which a
Newsman undergoes in attending to this department of his business, it will be necessary to
inform the reader, that he has perhaps thirty or

forty papers in circulation in this way at the same time; each of which papers must be transferred at the proper time from the residence of one reader to that of another. I believe that, in many cases, a Newsman or his boy will call at from seventy to eighty houses in this way, before four o'clock. I knew one boy who was in the habit, day after day, of calling at no fewer than one hundred and twenty places before that hour, to transfer the morning papers from one reader to another. It is but right, however, to state, that in this case the residences were less widely scattered than usual, otherwise it would have been impossible for any pair of human legs extant, to have accomplished the task.

I have mentioned an hour as the time the readers, to whom I have referred, keep the papers. That is usually the time; but agreements are often entered into between gentlemen and the Newsmen for a longer use of the journals. This is, perhaps, the most profitable part of the Newsmen's business. But for the money they obtain in this way, very few of them would get the thing to answer at all. The papers, after being thus read by a number of persons, are sent by that evening's post to the subscribers in the country, generally at the reduced price of fourpence. Formerly, when the price of a newspaper was sevenpence, twopence were deducted from the price paid by country subscribers for papers which were thus read in London; and as the papers are always kept clean, and persons in the country receive them at precisely the same time as if they had been put into the post-office the moment they come out of the hands of the printer, of course their being read in London makes no difference.

The laboriousness of this part of a Newsman's duties, considered only in reference to the extent of ground over which he has to go in a given time, will at once be seen to be sufficiently great. But bad as it is, it is not the worst circumstance in his lot. If there be an individual in Christendom who is entitled, in a special manner, to speak as one having authority touching the impossibility of pleasing everybody, it is the hapless vendor of the broad

sheet. He calls for the paper at the expiration
of the time allowed one gentleman for reading
it: the gentleman is of indolent, easy habits,
and has not perhaps opened it, and all the
proofs in the world will not persuade him that
he has yet had it half his regular time. He
then takes it up to read its contents, telling the
Newsman or Newsman's boy, either to wait in
the kitchen till he has done, or call again.
Another gentleman is a downright Tory, and he
is in the middle of a speech, of three or four
columns' length, of Lord Lyndhurst or Sir
Robert Peel; the Newsman might as soon ask
him for his purse, as ask him for the paper
before he has finished reading the Tory oration.
A third reader is a Liberal; and Lord Melbourne or Lord John Russell has brought a bill
into either of the Houses, as the case chances
to be, for the Municipal Corporation Reform in
Ireland, or for the Abolition of Church Rates
in England. A lengthened debate very naturally ensues thereon: the *Liberal* reader could
no more think of parting with the paper than
he could with the coat on his back, until he

sees under what monstrous pretext the Tories
can have the assurance to object to a measure
so demonstrably beneficial in its tendency. A
message is again sent up-stairs by the Newsman, that the time is up and that he cannot
wait any longer, as the paper has to be read by
other gentlemen. The party orders the servant
out of the room, and very likely calls her, if a
female, a hussey into the bargain: if a male
servant, he is threatened with a breakage of his
bones if he do not get down stairs directly.
The servant, whether male or female, goes down
and reproaches the ill-fated Newsman with
being the cause of putting "master" in a passion, and getting "people" into trouble: the
Newsman replies, in self-defence, that he shall
find himself "in trouble" with the next customer he has to go to, and that he *must* have
the paper. An angry altercation takes place
betwixt him and the servant, the latter peremptorily refusing to go up stairs again and make
"master" worse.

While this squabble is going on, "master"
comes and throws the paper down stairs, grow-

ling out, " Here, give it him." The servant
takes the journal, which was the innocent cause
of all this bickering and ill-blood, pokes it into
the Newsman's hand, and slams the door in
his face. He proceeds to the next reader.
The latter knew that a debate on a particular
subject, in which he felt a deep interest, was
expected to come on the previous night; or
whether it was so or not, he can no more live
without his broad sheet at the usual hour in the
morning, than he could, with any comfort to
himself, without his breakfast. Not a minute
has elapsed beyond the usual time for receiving
the journal he patronises, before he rings the
bell and asks Sally whether the Newsman has
arrived. Sally, especially if the gentleman be
a bachelor, simpers out in her most pleasant
manner, " I'se not a-seen him yet, sir."

" Oh! he's a lazy dog : Sally, be sure you
bring me up the paper the moment it arrives."

" I will, sir," answers the latter, making her
exit and shutting the door behind her.

" It's very provoking that the rascal should
be so much beyond his proper time," mutters

the gentleman to himself, taking a chair and
advancing towards the fire, if in the winter season; if in the summer season, seating himself
on the sofa.   A few minutes more expire, which
the gentleman magnifies into so many hours.
He rings the bell again with redoubled violence.
Her maidship quits the kitchen in, as she herself would say, "less than no time," and bounds
up stairs.   "No appearance of that fellow of a
Newsman yet, Sally?" growls the former, taking
three or four hasty steps through the room.

    " No, sir, he aint a-come yet."

    " Just look out at the door, and see if he be
coming."

    " I will, sir."

And down stairs Sally trips, with all due expedition, in order to ascertain whether the poor
Newsman may be descried from the street-
door; but just as she is putting her fingers to
the latchet to open it, a sudden and smart pull
of the bell causes so violent a clanging in her
ears that, taken quite by surprise and *half*
frightened to boot, she puts her hand to her
breast, and, as if almost suffocated, mutters

out—"A mercy on us! what's that?" The surprise and the fright, however, are only momentary: they have disappeared long before the bell has ceased to ring, and opening the door, she looks ominously at the Newsman, and, as she takes the paper out of his hand, observes, in her own peculiar way, " Oh, master is in *such* a rage at your being so late."

" I can't help it: it's not my fault," says the poor Newsman, in self-defence, literally gasping for breath, owing to his having run all the way from his last customer's residence.

" Oh, master don't care whose fault it is; he is *so* angry."

" I'm very sorry, but the fault——"

" I tell you what it is, sir," shouts a gruff voice from the first landing, before the hapless Newsman could finish his exculpatory sentence, " I tell you what it is, sir, if you can't bring the paper at the proper time I must employ some other person who will: that's all."

" Master," recognizing the Newsman's ring, had reached the top of the first pair of stairs in time to interrupt the dialogue between Sally and the vender of the broad sheet.

" I assure you, sir, that if——"

The Newsman renews his effort to explain in the best way he can the cause of the delay, but is interrupted again by his cross and crusty customer telling him that he will hear no excuse, but that if he is even a moment past his time again he need not bring the paper at all.

Incidents of this kind are matters of daily occurrence in the Newsman's eventful life. Very often, indeed, such incidents repeatedly occur in one day; for if the first or second of the readers detain the paper beyond the usual time, all who follow insist that they shall severally have out their allowed time, without reference to the time at which they got it.

When this portion of the Newsman's duties are over, he has next either to go himself, or send one of his boys, to the Courier office, to dispose of any of the morning papers he has on hand. If there be a demand for any particular journal to supply the country customers of other Newsmen, and such journal is not to be

had at the office of publication, then the Newsman having that journal to dispose of will get
full price for it. If the supply considerably
exceeds the demand, in consequence of several
Newsmen having taken more copies in the
morning than they could dispose of, then there
is a proportionate reduction in the price. Opposite the door of the Courier office, has been
for more than a quarter of a century the only
locality recognised by Newsmen for disposing
among each other of their over supplies of morning papers. What led to its being first fixed
on for that purpose, I cannot say; very probably it may have been its central situation.
This particular traffic in the morning journals
usually begins at four o'clock, and is in most
cases over by five. In the majority of cases
the Newsmen, instead of going themselves,
send their boys to transact this part of their
business; and right noisy little fellows they are.
Some time ago they were so uproarious and
blocked up the passage on the pavement so
completely, that it was deemed requisite to
station a policeman at the place to maintain

something like order. It is often amusing to
hear them proclaiming aloud the various newspapers they have for sale. "Who's got a
'*Eral* or a *Chron.?*" "Who's for a '*Tiser* or
Toimes?" shouts one little fellow in the same
breath. "I've got a '*Eral*," answers one.
"Here's a *Chron.*," answers another. A third
sings out, "I'll take a '*Tiser*," and a fourth
bawls, at the full stretch of his voice, "I vants
a *Toimes*," elbowing his way through the
crowd towards the party having the paper to
dispose of. But to form anything like a correct idea of the scene which is every afternoon
exhibited at the Courier office, you must fancy
that you hear scores of voices all shouting out
something of the kind I have mentioned, at
once, and where you see scores of boys pushing
one another backwards and forwards, and playing all description of tricks.

Here let me remark, by way of parenthesis,
that since this was written, a great part of the
business done in this way has been removed to
the bottom of Catherine Street; which, as
my town readers are aware, is only about

twelve or fifteen yards from the Courier-office.
I have not heard the cause of this removal.

Between four and five comes the publication
of the evening papers, which now occupies the
attention of the Newsmen. In this case, however, their pedestrian capabilities are not called
into exercise to the same extent as in the case of
the morning papers, the far greater portion of
the evening journals being simply put into the
post-office, to be forwarded to subscribers in the
country. The delivery of the evening papers is
usually over before six o'clock; but then, for at
least six months in the year, that is to say,
during the time that Parliament is sitting, they
have to watch the publications of second editions of the evening papers, as many of their
country customers give positive instructions to
have the second editions regularly sent to
them.

Some idea may be formed from what I have
stated of the laboriousness of a Newsman's life.
If there be an industrious hard-working member
of the community, he is the man. I am assured that there are some Newsmen who, in the

prosecution of their pursuits as distributors of
the public journals, walk or run upwards of
twenty miles every day.   And this, be it recol-
lected, in all weathers, whether in the "summer's heat" or the "winter's cold."

And what aggravates the hardship of the
Newsman's condition is, that the Sabbath, which
to most other classes of the community affords
a cessation from labour, "shines no day of rest
to him."   A considerable part of that day is
spent in the delivery of the Sunday papers.

And yet, notwithstanding the laborious duties
which devolve on the Newsman, and the fact
that he scarcely ever enjoys one hour's intermission from one year's end to another; notwithstanding this, his remuneration is so small,
after paying the necessary expenses incurred in
carrying on his business, and allowing for bad
debts and unsold papers, that, except in very rare
cases indeed, he has no prospect, by any prac-
ticable economy, of ever being able to "lay
by" anything against the time of sickness or
the infirmities of advanced years : and he thinks
it a great matter if he can by his utmost industry

and exertions, earn as much as will procure him
his daily bread.

I know of no body of men who contribute
more largely to the comfort of the metropolitan
community than the Newsmen. Without them
the daily papers could not be expeditiously or
effectually circulated throughout so vast a place
as London. I cannot conceive of any machinery, were the task of distributing their
papers left to the proprietors of the papers
themselves, by which that task could be satis-
factorily executed. Whenever any country
order for a newspaper is addressed to the proprietors of the paper ordered, which is often
done through ignorance of the fact that all the
London journals are circulated through the
intervention of Newsmen, the order is handed
over to some particular Newsman, and, for the
penny profit on each copy of the paper, he runs
the risk of the bad debt, should there be no
order for payment on any house in London.

There are, as before-mentioned, three or four
wholesale news-agents in London. They supply the Newsmen whose business is not so large

as to justify them in ordering quires at a time of particular journals. They supply them on the same terms as if they had gone for any quantity under a quire, to the office of the paper, their own profit consisting in the odd paper given them gratis by the publishers after every quire they order. Those Newsmen in the habit of using a quire of any particular journal make a point of going direct to the office of publication, because they are also entitled to the odd paper after every quire. Some of the wholesale news-paper agents pass an incredible number of newspapers through their hands in one day. I have heard the number which passes through the hand of one house estimated at seven thou-sand per day. These wholesale Newsmen have very extensive country connexions, and send off newspapers by the morning coaches in thousands to all parts of the country.

Most of the Newsmen keep small shops for carrying on their business, and most of them deal, in addition to the newspapers, in cheap periodicals and other publications.

PRINTED BY STEWART AND MURRAY, OLD BAILEY.